TORNADOES

DANGEROUS WEATHER

TORNADOES

Michael Allaby

Facts On File, Inc.

Facts On File, Inc.
11 Penn Plaza
New York NY 10001

Library of Congress Cataloging-in-Publication Data
Allaby, Michael.

    Tornadoes / Michael Allaby.
        p.   cm. — (Dangerous weather)
    Includes index.
    ISBN 0-8160-3517-2 (acid-free paper)
    1. Tornadoes. I. Title. II. Series: Allaby, Michael. Dangerous
weather.
    QC955.A45   1997
    551.55′3—dc20   96-20742

Facts On File books are available at special discounts when purchased in bulk quantities for businesses, associations, institutions or sales promotions. Please call our Special Sales Department in New York at (212) 967-8800 or (800) 322-8755.

You can find Facts On File on the World Wide Web at http://www.factsonfile.com

Text design by Richard Garratt
Cover design by Matt Galemmo
Illustrations by Richard Garratt

Printed in the United States of America

RRD FOF 10 9 8 7 6 5 4

This book is printed on acid-free paper.

CONTENTS

TORNADOES

What is a tornado?

All morning the air over the plain feels heavy, oppressive, and hot. It is almost difficult to breathe. By noon a strong breeze is blowing from the south, but it brings little relief from the sweltering heat. As the afternoon wears on, the sky begins to cloud over from the west, with sheets of thin, white, very high cloud that gradually merge into a continuous cover.

Far away, scientists studying satellite photographs have spotted a line of thunderstorms developing and are gathering as much information about them as they can from ground observers, aircraft, and radar. Already they have broadcast warnings of approaching storms to people in their path.

Behind the white cloud, in the far distance, the western horizon darkens. A storm is on its way, and by 3 P.M. people going about their everyday business are pausing now and then to glance nervously at what now appears as a solid wall of dark cloud moving rapidly toward them. This cloud seems to extend from the ground to as high as anyone can see. In fact, its base is a few hundred feet above the ground and its top at about 50,000 feet. Here and there the cloud wall flickers as lightning flashes to and fro inside it, and

Figure 1: *Tornado in Alfalfa, Oklahoma, May 22, 1981.* (National Severe Storms Laboratory, NOAA)

as it comes closer lightning can be seen streaking to the ground. Radio stations continue to broadcast warnings.

Overhead, the cloud thickens and hail begins to fall. Driven by winds that are now fierce, hailstones, some the size of golf balls, send everyone running for shelter. The noise is almost deafening as they batter into buildings and cars parked in the street.

Then the hail eases, as though the storm is passing, but the first sign emerges of the real menace. At the base of the cloud to the southwest there seem to be fragments traveling in opposite directions. Soon it is clear they are the same fragments, moving fast in a tight circle. Probably they are about two miles away, but there is no way of estimating their size, so it is difficult to tell. The twirling cloud descends from the cloud base, like a white funnel, until it reaches the ground. Then its color starts to change. A cloud of darker material surrounds its base, then extends upward, darkening the entire column. With a deep roar, the column is moving northeast, straight for the town. Scientists tracking it measure its speed as 45 MPH. By the time it arrives, everyone has taken shelter in the safest places they could find.

This is a tornado, or twister, or whirlwind. It may live no longer than half an hour, often less but occasionally for longer, and it is no more than half a mile wide at the base. Yet this is by far the most ferocious storm known on Earth. During its short life it will expend about as much energy as is used to light all the streets of New York City for one night. Inside it, the wind blows at never less than 90 MPH, sometimes at speeds approaching 300 MPH, and it blows in an upward spiral, lifting dust, dirt, and loose material and carrying it aloft.

Its destructive power is immense. In April 1974, a tornado destroyed 900 houses in the space of 20 minutes. On the same day, and in a shorter time than that, one damaged or demolished nearly 3,000 buildings in the city of Xenia, Ohio. It ripped away the top story of Xenia High School and dropped a bus onto the school stage. Tornadoes often form in groups and the storms that give rise to them move, sometimes rapidly, spawning tornadoes as they go. The 1974 Xenia tornado was one of what came to be called the "Super Outbreak." On April 3 and 4, 148 tornadoes were reported within 24 hours, affecting 13 U.S. states and Canada. In 16 hours and 10 minutes the storms traveled 2,598 miles.

Tornadoes can form at any time of year and any time of day or night, but they are more likely at certain times. In the United States there are more between April and June and two-thirds develop in the afternoon and early evening, one-quarter of all tornadoes striking between 4 P.M. and 6 P.M.

More tornadoes occur in the United States than anywhere else in the world, but they are common in many countries. It seems they are rare in Africa and India, although not unknown. On January 8, 1993, a tornado killed 32 people and injured more than 1,000 in Bangladesh, and on April 9 of the same year one destroyed five villages and killed 100 people in West Bengal. There are approximately 60 each year in Britain. Most go unreported, because they affect open farmland where no one sees them and British people do not expect them. The many references to "whirlwinds" in the Old Testament show that in the Near East people have long been familiar with tornadoes and think of them as the most destructive forces imaginable.

When warm and cold air collide

Tornadoes grow out of extremely violent thunderstorms, and thunderstorms develop in air that is highly unstable. "Stable" air lies in layers, like those in a cake. Winds may blow through it horizontally, but there is little or no vertical movement of air. In stable air as in layer cakes, the layers do not mix. If something forces the air to rise, when it crosses hills, for example, it sinks again as soon as the lifting force is removed. "Unstable" air is quite different. It rises and continues to rise until it reaches a level where the air above it is lighter than itself and it can rise no further. Sometimes the rising air can reach a very great height. That is what happens in a large storm (see page 30).

Stable and unstable air are obviously different. They possess certain characteristics that make them stable or unstable. This suggests that in some way there are different kinds of air. They do not differ chemically, of course. All air contains the same gases in the same proportions. The difference is in the amount of water vapor they contain, which can vary widely, and in their temperatures.

Think of what happens to air that stays in the same place for a few weeks. The Sun shines through it, warming the land or sea beneath the air, and the air is warmed by contact with the surface. Air is warmed from below, not from above. As it warms, water will evaporate into it, so it will hold water vapor, and the amount of water vapor that air can hold depends on the temperature. Warm air can hold more water vapor than cool air, and if moist air is cooled some of its water vapor condenses into droplets. This is why the windows steam up when you get into a car on a cold day. Your breath is warm and moist, but the windows are cold. When the warm breath reaches the windows it is cooled, so it is able to hold less water vapor and some condenses as droplets onto the windows.

Suppose the air lies over the ocean somewhere in the tropics. It will be heated strongly because it is in a warm place and there is plenty of water to evaporate into it. It will be warm, moist air. Now imagine the air sits for a time over northern Canada. It will be cold and dry. Large bodies of air that have remained in one place long

Air masses and the weather they bring

As air moves slowly across the surface it is sometimes warmed, sometimes cooled; in some places water evaporates into it, and in others it loses moisture. Its characteristics change.

When it crosses a very large region, such as a continent or ocean, its principal characteristics are evened out and over a vast area all the air is at much the same temperature and pressure and is equally moist or dry. Such a body of air is called an *air mass*.

Air masses are warm, cool, moist, or dry according to the region over which they formed, and are named accordingly. The names and their abbreviations are straightforward. Continental (c) air masses form over continents, maritime (m) ones over oceans. Depending on the latitude in which they form, air masses may be Arctic (A), polar (P), tropical (T), or equatorial (E). Except in the case of equatorial air, these categories are then combined to give continental Arctic (cA), maritime Arctic (mA), continental polar (cP), maritime polar (mP), continental tropical (cT), and maritime tropical (mT).

North America is affected by mP, cP, cT, and mT air, the maritime air masses originating over the Pacific, Atlantic, or Gulf. As they move from where they formed (called their *source regions*) air masses change, but they do so slowly and at first they bring with them the weather conditions that produced them. As their names suggest, maritime air is moist, continental air is dry, polar air is cool, and tropical air is warm. At the surface there is little difference between polar and Arctic air, but there are differences in the upper atmosphere.

It is cP air spilling south when the cT and mT move toward the equator in the fall that brings cold, dry winters to the central United States. It is the meeting of mT air from the Gulf and cT air from inland that produces fierce storms in the southeast of the country.

Air masses affecting North America.

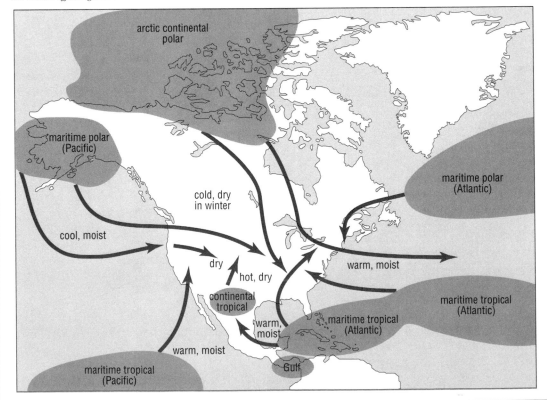

enough to become warm or cold, moist or dry, are called *air masses* (see box 1). As the map in box 1 shows, air masses of all the principal types form over North America.

Gases consist of molecules, which are atoms joined together. Nitrogen molecules comprise two nitrogen atoms (N–N, written as N_2), oxygen molecules two oxygen atoms (O–O, written as O_2), and between them nitrogen and oxygen make up about 99% of our air. Gas molecules move freely and at random. They dart here and there, hit one another, and bounce away in new directions. How fast they move depends on how much energy they have. If the gas, or air, is warmed, the heat increases their energy and makes them move faster. When they move faster they also move farther away from each other, and because they are farther apart, they occupy more space. In other words, when air is warmed it expands and when it is cooled it contracts. You can prove this for yourself with experiment 4 in volume 6.

Imagine one cubic foot of air. If you warm the air, the volume will increase, say to 2 cubic feet. The one cubic foot of cool air weighs the same as the 2 cubic feet of warm air because the two volumes contain the same quantity of air. If you weigh one cubic foot of cold air, warm all the air, then weigh one cubic foot of warm air, it will weigh less because some molecules have moved away, so the same volume contains less air. The same volumes of warm air and cold air contain different numbers of molecules; to put it another way, they are of different densities.

Place an inflated balloon in a full bathtub and it will float. If you want it to be at the bottom of the tub, you will have to push it down, and the moment you release it the balloon will bob to the surface. This is because the balloon contains air, which is less dense than water, and in gases and liquids, which allow free movement, less dense things rise above denser things. In ordinary air, less dense air will float to the top of denser air. Figure 2 shows that a bubble (meteorologists call it a "parcel of air") will rise if it contains fewer molecules than the surrounding air and so is less dense. Unstable air is less dense than the air above it, so it rises until it reaches a level where the surrounding air has the same density as itself.

Once it reaches this level it can rise no farther, and if the air settles (with less dense air overlying denser air), it will become stable. After that, there will be very little mixing. It is difficult to demonstrate this with air, but water behaves in the same way and experiment 10 in volume 6 should convince you.

Air masses, each with their own distinct characteristics, form all over the world. Then, slowly but not all at the same speed, they drift away from where they originated. Where two air masses with different densities meet they mix very slowly. A boundary, or *front*, forms between them (see box on page 6), where warm, less dense air rises over the cooler, denser air. This reluctance of

Figure 2: *Less dense air will rise through denser air.*

Weather fronts

During the First World War, the Norwegian meteorologist Vilhelm Bjerknes (see volume 6 for biographical details) discovered that air forms distinct masses. Because each mass differs in its average temperature, and therefore density, from adjacent masses, air masses do not mix readily. He called the boundary between two air masses a *front*.

Air masses move across the surface of land and sea, and so the fronts between them also move. Fronts are named according to the temperature of the air *behind* the front compared with that ahead of it. If the air behind the advancing front is warmer than the air ahead of it, it is a *warm front*. If the air behind the front is cooler, it is a *cold front*.

Fronts extend from the surface all the way to the tropopause, which is the boundary between the lower (troposphere) and upper (stratosphere) layers of the atmosphere. They slope upward, like the sides of a bowl, but the slope is very shallow. Warm fronts have a gradient of 1° or less, cold fronts of about 2°. (These gradients are greatly exaggerated below.)

Cold fronts usually move faster across the surface of land than warm fronts, so cold air tends to undercut warm air, raising it upward along the edge of the cold front. If warm air is

Frontal depressions.
1. Ana-front (air rising along both fronts). 2. Kata-front (air sinking along both fronts).

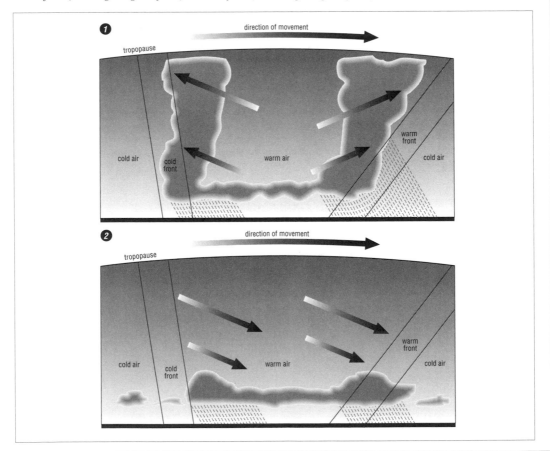

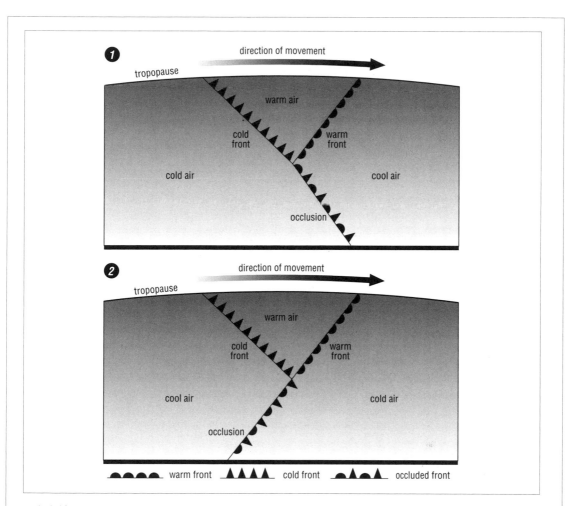

Occluded fronts.

rising, it will be raised even faster along the front separating it from cold air. The cold front is then called an *ana-front* and there is usually thick cloud and heavy rain or snow. If the warm air is sinking, an advancing cold front will raise it less. This is a *kata-front,* usually with only low-level cloud and light rain, drizzle, or fine snow.

After a front has formed, waves start to develop along it. These are shown on weather maps and as they become steeper, areas of low pressure form at their crests. These are frontal *depressions,* which often bring wet weather. Just below the wave crest, there is cold air to either side of a body of warm air. The cold front moves faster than the warm front, lifting the warm air along both fronts

until all the warm air is clear of the surface. The fronts are then said to be *occluded* and the pattern they form is called an *occlusion*.

Once the fronts are occluded and the warm air is no longer in contact with the surface, air to both sides of the occlusion is colder than the warm air. Occlusions can still be called cold or warm, however, because what matters is not the actual temperature of the air, but whether air to one side of a front or occlusion is warmer or cooler than the air behind it. In a cold occlusion the air ahead of the front is warmer than the air behind it and in a warm occlusion the air ahead is cooler.

masses of air of different densities to mix is what produces a great deal of the weather we experience day by day.

Clouds often form along fronts as warm air rises and its water vapor condenses (see box on page 32 for an explanation of why this happens). Occasionally, though, the effect can be much more dramatic. It sometimes happens that cold air moves beneath very warm, very moist air. The warm air may have been stable, with little or no vertical movement taking place within it. Now, however, it is forced to rise and this destabilizes it. Once it starts rising it continues to do so and strong vertical currents develop inside it as air rises, cools, sinks, then rises again. These are the conditions that can generate towering storm clouds. If they are big enough, violent enough, and there is something to start the air turning, tornadoes may form below them.

Figure 3: *Meeting of air masses that produces storms.*

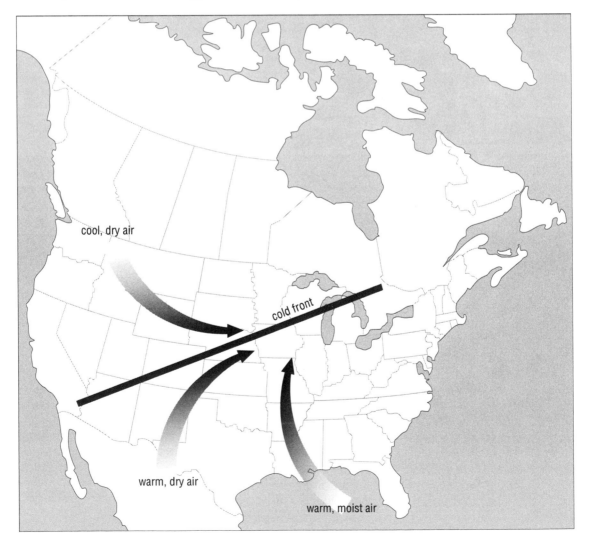

cool, dry air

cold front

warm, dry air

warm, moist air

These circumstances can and do arise anywhere, but the most violent storms of all arise when more than two air masses collide. This happens fairly often over North America in spring and summer, in the situation illustrated in figure 3.

One air mass has moved southeastward from the North Pacific, crossed the coast in British Columbia, then crossed the Rockies and entered North Dakota. Maritime polar (mP) air, it is cold and moist when it crosses the coast. As it rises over the mountains it loses its moisture, so to the east of the Rockies it is dry, but still cold.

A second air mass is moving north from central Mexico. It has spent time over the desert and is warm, dry, continental tropical (cT) air. It meets the cold mP air in the central United States, at a front running from southwest to northeast, approximately along the line of the jet stream (see page 16). There, the warm air moving north rises over the cold air.

Air is also moving northwest from the Gulf of Mexico. This is maritime tropical (mT) air, very warm and very moist, and it meets the other two air masses at the front. This is a cold front, moving in a southeasterly direction.

Along its way north, the cT air from Mexico crosses the warm ground of the southern states, which helps it retain its heat, meets the advancing cold air, which is denser, and rises over it. Both air masses are dry, so the front produces little or no clouds. The weather is fine below and to either side of it.

Then the mT air arrives from the Gulf. It also crosses warm ground, and because in spring and summer the sea is usually cooler than the land, its temperature may rise. It is only slightly unstable until it meets the cold front, but there it is forced to rise and this greatly increases its instability. Heaped clouds develop, it starts to rain, and there may be some thunderstorms.

Were it not for the cT air from Mexico, the rain and thunderstorms would be the only results of the cold front. The cT air forms a layer of stable air the rising mT air cannot penetrate, trapping the warm Gulf air between the cold air below and warm air above and preventing it from dissipating all its heat.

At the top of the "sandwich," the Mexican cT air is cooling, however, and a point is reached at which Gulf air starts to rise through it. This abruptly releases all the energy of the warm, moist air, producing vertical air currents and clouds extending almost from ground level to the tropopause, the boundary between the lower atmosphere (called the troposphere) and the stratosphere, at a height of about 50,000 feet. Now the storms become really spectacular, with lightning, thunder, torrential rain, and hail. If the jet stream, just above the cloud tops, sets the air twisting, the huge storm clouds may generate tornadoes.

How wind changes with height

Huge thunderstorms are necessary for tornadoes to develop, but by themselves they are not enough. The wind near the cloud tops must blow from a different direction than the wind lower down. This change in direction is needed to disperse high-level air and set the air at lower levels spinning.

It is quite usual for the wind at high level to blow from a different direction and at a different speed from the wind we experience on the ground. You can sometimes see this when clouds, carried by the wind, move across the sky in a different direction from the way a wind vane is pointing.

Before they take off on long flights, pilots check the weather along their routes. In particular, they are interested in the strength and direction of the winds they will encounter. Using up-to-date tables showing the winds at different heights, pilots determine the altitude with the most favorable wind, to increase speed over the ground and conserve fuel.

Air moves away from areas of high pressure and toward areas of low pressure, its strength depending on the difference in pressure between the two areas. This is called the *pressure gradient* (see box on 12) and it is what causes the wind. Because it results from a pressure gradient, it is called the *gradient wind.*

If you calculate from the pressure gradient what the strength of the gradient wind should be, you will find the wind strength at ground level is different. Near the ground, friction with trees, buildings, and the ground surface itself slows the wind, and as it flows and eddies around obstructions the wind changes direction as well as speed. At weather stations, the surface wind is measured by instruments sited well clear of obstructions and a standard 33 feet above the ground. Wind at higher levels is measured by releasing balloons and tracking them with binoculars or by radio.

Friction is greater over dry land than over the sea, so the wind is always stronger at sea than it is over land. Also, because there are no obstructions at sea, its direction is more constant and closer to that indicated by the pressure gradient.

Wind strength increases with height because the higher you climb the smaller the influence of friction. The layer of air in which friction significantly affects the wind is known as the *surface* (or *turbulent*) *boundary layer.* Its depth is variable, but it usually extends some 150 to 3,000 feet above the surface. Above the surface boundary layer the gradient wind is called the *geostrophic wind.*

Wind does not flow directly from high to low pressure. The rotation of the Earth deflects air moving above it. This was first

Air pressure, highs, and lows

When air is warmed it expands and becomes less dense. When air is chilled it contracts and becomes more dense.

Air expands by pushing away the air around it. It rises because it is less dense than the air immediately above it. Denser air flows in to replace it, is warmed by contact with the surface, and also expands and rises. Imagine a column of air extending all the way from the surface to the top of the atmosphere. Warming from below causes expansion; as a result, some air is pushed out of the column, so the remaining air is less dense (contains fewer molecules of air) than it was when it was cooler. Because there is less air in the column, the pressure its weight exerts at the surface is reduced. The result is an area of low surface pressure, often called simply a *low*.

In chilled air the opposite happens. The air molecules move closer together, so the air contracts, becomes more dense, and sinks. The amount of air in the column increases, its weight increases, and the surface atmospheric pressure also increases. This produces an area of high pressure, or simply a *high*.

At sea level, the atmosphere exerts sufficient pressure to raise a column of mercury about 30 inches (760 mm) in a tube from which the air has been removed. Meteorologists call this pressure one *bar* and measure atmospheric pressure in *millibars* (1,000 millibar (mb) = 1 bar = 10^6 dynes cm^{-2} = 101,325 pascals).

Air pressure decreases with height because there is less air above to exert pressure. Pressure measured at different places on the surface is corrected to sea-level pressure to remove differences due only to altitude. Lines are then drawn linking places where the pressure is the same. These lines, called *isobars*, allow meteorologists to study the distribution of pressure.

Like water flowing downhill, air flows from high to low pressure. Its speed, which we feel as wind strength, depends on the difference in pressure between the two regions. This is called the *pressure gradient*. On a weather map it is calculated from the distance between isobars, just as the distance between contours on an ordinary map allows the steepness of hills to be measured. The steeper the gradient the stronger the wind.

Moving air experiences friction with the surface. This slows it more over land, where the friction is greater, than over the sea. Air is also subject to the Coriolis effect, which swings it to the right in the northern hemisphere and to the left in the southern hemisphere. As a consequence, winds do not cross the isobars at 90°. Over the oceans they cross at about 30° and over land at about 45°.

Pressure gradient and wind speed (pressures in millibars).

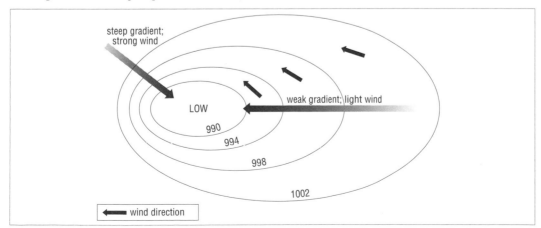

Christoph Buys Ballot and his law

In 1857, the Dutch meteorologist Christoph Buys Ballot (see volume 6 for a biographical note) published a summary of his observations on the relationship between atmospheric pressure and wind. He had concluded that in the northern hemisphere winds flow counterclockwise around area of low pressure and clockwise around areas of high pressure. In the southern hemisphere these directions are reversed.

Unknown to Buys Ballot, a few months earlier the American meteorologist William Ferrel had applied the laws of physics and calculated this would be the case. Buys Bal-

Buys Ballot's law: In the northern hemisphere, winds flow in a clockwise direction around centers of high pressure and counterclockwise around centers of low pressure. Therefore, if you stand with your back to the wind the center of low pressure is to your left. In the southern hemisphere these directions are reversed.

lot acknowledged Ferrel's prior claim to the discovery, but despite this, the phenomenon is now known as *Buys Ballot's law*. This states that, in the northern hemisphere, if you stand with your back to the wind the area of low pressure is to your left and the area of high pressure to your right. In the southern hemisphere, if you stand with your back to the wind the area of low pressure is to your right and the area of high pressure to your left. (The law does not apply very close to the equator.)

The law is a consequence of the combined effect of the *pressure-gradient force* (PGF) and the *Coriolis effect* or *Coriolis force* (CorF). Air flows from an area of high pressure to one of low pressure, like water flowing downhill. Just as the speed of flowing water depends on the steepness of the slope (the gradient), so the speed of flowing air depends on the difference in pressure between high and low (the PGF).

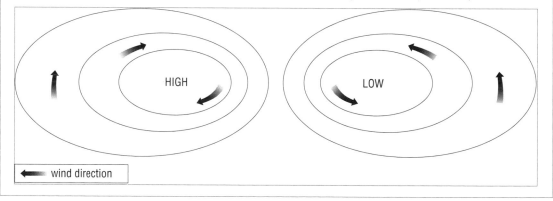

HIGH

LOW

wind direction

explained by the French physicist Gaspard Gustave de Coriolis and came to be called the *Coriolis force*, abbreviated as CorF (see box on page 50). The abbreviation is still used, but CorF is no longer thought of as a force, because nothing pushes the wind to deflect it. What Coriolis discovered was simply the consequence of air (or water, as ocean currents) moving in relation to the Earth (which also moves) but as seen by an observer in a fixed position in relation to the solid Earth. It is an effect, not a force, and today it is called the *Coriolis effect*.

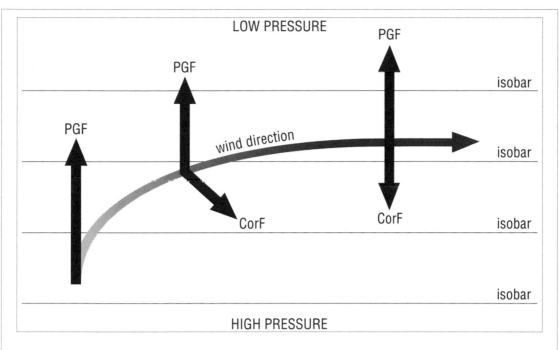

LOW PRESSURE

PGF

PGF

PGF

PGF

isobar

wind direction

isobar

CorF

CorF

isobar

isobar

HIGH PRESSURE

The geostrophic wind.

As the air flows, the CorF, acting at right angles to the direction of flow, swings it to the right in the northern hemisphere and to the left in the southern hemisphere. As it starts to swing to the right, the CorF and PGF produce a resultant force that accelerates it. CorF is proportional to the speed of the moving air, so it increases, swinging the air still more to the right. This continues until the air is flowing parallel to the isobars (at right angles to the pressure gradient). At this point, the PGF and CorF are acting in opposite directions. If the PGF is the stronger force, the air will swing to the left and accelerate. This will increase the CorF, swinging it back to the right again. If the CorF is the stronger, the air will swing farther to the right, the PGF acting in the opposite direction will slow it, the CorF will decrease, and the air will swing to the left again. The eventual result is to make the air flow parallel to the isobars (pressure gradient) rather than across them.

Near the ground, friction with the surface and objects on it slow the air, acting as an additional force. This deflects the air so it flows at an angle to the isobars, rather than parallel to them. Clear of the surface, the air does flow parallel to the isobars. This is called the *geostrophic wind*.

Air moves at all because of a pressure gradient. This is a real force, called the pressure-gradient force (PGF). CorF counters the PGF as though it were a force acting in the opposite direction. The direction of the resulting gradient wind is determined by the relative strengths of these two components. It was a Dutch meteorologist, Christoph Buys Ballot, who, in 1857, first described what actually happens. His result is summarized as *Buys Ballot's law* (see box on page 12), which states that in the northern hemisphere, winds flow counterclockwise around areas of low pressure and clockwise around areas of high pressure (in the southern hemisphere these directions are reversed).

Seen looking down from above the North Pole, the Earth rotates counterclockwise and this also has an effect. Winds flowing in a clockwise direction are moving in the opposite direction to the Earth's rotation and this tends to slow them. This means that, in the northern hemisphere, winds around areas of high pressure are usually weaker than those around areas of low pressure.

Friction slows the wind in the surface boundary layer. This affects the balance between the PGF and CorF, making the wind flow more in the direction of the pressure gradient. At the Earth's surface, over land the wind is deflected by about 25–35° in the direction of the low-pressure region and over sea by 10–20°. With increasing height, the effect of friction diminishes until the wind direction is that of the geostrophic wind, but this happens gradually. Instead of a sudden transition from the gradient wind to the geostrophic wind, wind direction describes a spiral. Wind-driven ocean currents behave in the same way, their direction changing with increasing depth. This was first discovered in 1905, by a Swedish oceanographer, Vagn Walfrid Ekman (1874–1954). It is known as an *Ekman spiral* whether it occurs in the ocean or the atmosphere (see volume 6 for more details). During their climb, pilots may need to take account of changing wind direction due to the Ekman spiral.

If that were all they had to worry about, air navigation would be a great deal simpler than it is. Modern aircraft climb fast enough for the spiraling change in low-level wind direction to have no significant effect on them. All the pilot would need to know is the wind at cruising height.

Sometimes this is enough, but more often it is not. CorF is greatest at the North and South Pole and close to zero near the equator. This causes wind speeds to decrease the farther air moves away from the equator. The PGF that produces a wind of 34 MPH at 43° latitude, for example, will produce only a 23-MPH wind at 90°. So, regardless of altitude, the wind speed changes with latitude.

Remember, too, that the wind flows around centers of high and low pressure. An aircraft flying across a pressure system will, therefore, experience wind blowing first from one direction, then the center itself where winds are light, and finally wind blowing from the opposite direction. Drift caused by the first may be corrected by opposite drift from the last, but then again it may not.

It will not if the aircraft flies through a weather front (see box on page 6). The aircraft shown in figure 4 is about to fly through a warm front. The lower part of the drawing shows its position as this might appear on a weather map. It is flying into a headwind caused by the clockwise flow around the high-pressure center. The location of the front on the ground does not agree with its location at the height of the aircraft, however, because the front slopes, as though the cold air were held beneath an inverted bowl. The aircraft is about to meet the front, and as it crosses, the headwind will become a tail wind.

Consider now the situation as seen by a person standing on the ground watching the plane fly overhead. The surface wind is blowing in one direction. Above the surface, just clear of the surface boundary layer, it is blowing in another direction and more strongly.

Figure 4: *Change in wind direction with height.*

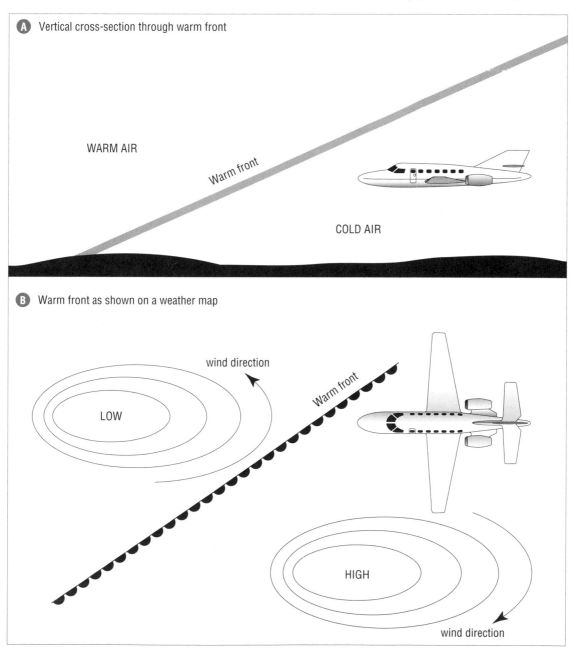

A Vertical cross-section through warm front

WARM AIR

Warm front

COLD AIR

B Warm front as shown on a weather map

wind direction

LOW

Warm front

HIGH

wind direction

Above that again there is another wind blowing in the opposite direction and, in all likelihood, at a different speed.

More often than not, the wind varies considerably with increasing height. Moving upward through the surface boundary layer, the speed increases and direction changes through an Ekman spiral as the gradient wind becomes the geostrophic wind. Higher still, the pressure regime may change, with a corresponding change in wind direction and strength. Some hundreds of miles ahead of the surface location of an advancing warm front or behind a retreating cold front, low-level high pressure will lie beneath low pressure, the altitude of the transition depending on distance from the surface position of the front and its angle of slope.

Most weather systems, but especially tornadoes, arise from interactions between atmospheric conditions at low and high levels. In the case of tornadoes, it is necessary for the high-level wind to blow strongly from a different direction to that of the wind at low and medium heights. It is no coincidence, therefore, that tornadoes often occur where air masses meet at fronts or that many of them form beneath the strongest of all high-level winds, the Polar Front Jet stream, associated with the Polar Front.

Jet streams

During the 1940s the performance of aircraft improved dramatically. Planes flew faster, farther, and higher than older models. For the first time, some flew regularly at altitudes of 30,000 feet or more, where the air is so thin it offers less resistance than air lower down, so planes use less fuel.

It was while they were flying at these heights that pilots began to notice something curious. Despite the wind predictions they were given before takeoff, occasionally westward journeys took much longer than they had calculated and on eastward journeys they arrived ahead of schedule. They concluded there must sometimes be a very powerful wind at these heights. It was not always in the same place, or there at all, but it usually blew in a generally westerly direction (from west to east). They had discovered a wind blowing like the exhaust jet from a jet airplane, and it came to be called the *jet stream*.

Occasionally, the jet stream reveals itself to people on the ground. If you see long lines of cloud at a very great height, rather like vapor trails but longer and forming parallel streaks, they may have been blown into this shape by the jet stream.

The jet stream is a narrow band of wind at around 30,000 feet. It is stronger and farther south in winter than in summer. Figure 5A shows its usual location over North America in January and figure 5B shows it in July. The drawing shows it blowing at 95 MPH, but in winter it can be much stronger than this, often exceeding 100 MPH and sometimes reaching 300 MPH. It is easy to see how a wind of this force would affect journey times. It is also easy to see how the jet stream can provide the wind, blowing in a different direction from winds at lower altitudes, needed to set the air below it spinning to trigger tornadoes.

It also has another important effect. Frontal systems (see box on page 6) tend to develop beneath it. Since these can cause severe thunderstorms, the jet stream is associated with storms big enough to generate tornadoes; it also provides the mechanism to set rising air spinning.

Although it blows from a generally westerly direction, the jet stream is not constant. Indeed, it is a little misleading to think of "the" jet stream at all, because there can be several in different places at the same time. The principal jet stream over North America and Europe is the Polar Front Jet Stream, but there is also a Subtropical Jet Stream nearer the equator and in summer an Easterly Tropical Jet Stream occurs over Africa and India. The Subtropical Jet Stream is more constant than the Polar Front Jet Stream, but weaker. As its name suggests, the Easterly Tropical Jet Stream blows from an easterly direction (from east to west).

Figure 5 a: *Jet stream position in January.*

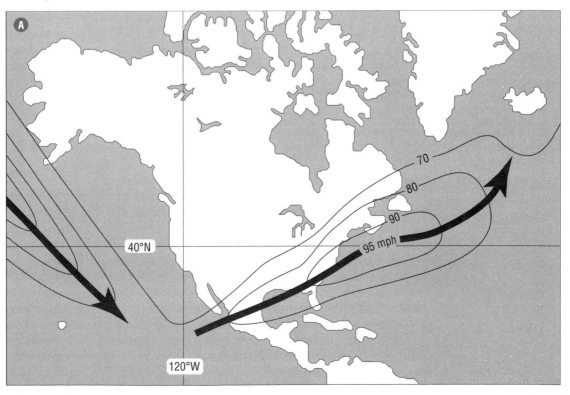

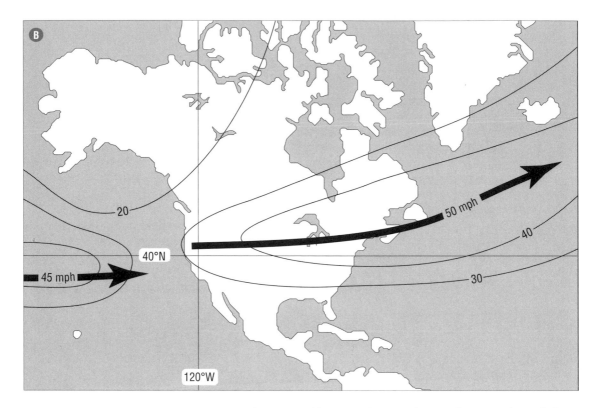

Figure 5 b: *Jet stream position in July.*

Air moving horizontally over the Earth's surface tends to follow a curved path, as though it were rotating about a vertical axis through its center. This tendency to rotate is called *vorticity* (see page 48). It is due to the movement of the air in relation to the Earth's own movement, so it is greatest at the equator, where the surface of the Earth is moving fastest. Moving air is also subject to the Coriolis effect (see box on page 50), which is weakest at the equator and strongest at the poles.

The Polar Front Jet Stream flows from west to east, but is readily diverted toward the north or south. If it swings to the north, its own vorticity decreases and the Coriolis effect on it increases. This swings it to the south again, but then the Coriolis effect on it decreases and its own vorticity increases, swinging it back to the north. In this way the jet stream develops very long waves, often measuring more than 1,200 miles between crests. These were first discovered in 1940 by the Swedish-American meteorologist Carl-Gustav Rossby and they are known as *Rossby waves* (see volume 6 for more details).

In figure 5, the Polar Front Jet Stream swings south over North America as part of one of these waves. Swings toward the equator are called *troughs* and swings away from the equator *ridges*. The longer waves tend to remain stationary for most of the time, or sometimes move slowly westward. Shorter waves that form along the long waves travel eastward.

As the jet stream enters a trough, it narrows, accelerates, and air converges into it. Convergence at a high level produces an area of high pressure in the lower atmosphere. The stream widens and slows around the trough itself, then narrows and accelerates again as it approaches the ridge. This time, however, air diverges from it and the divergence produces an area of low pressure in the lower atmosphere. Undulations in the jet stream are responsible for much of our bad weather, and especially for storms.

Although the Rossby waves are fairly stable, from time to time they break down in a sequence of steps illustrated in figure 6. This happens when the jet stream and the westerly winds around it are to the north of their usual position. The sequence is called the *index cycle*, because the upper-atmosphere westerly winds are called *zonal* and their strength is known as the *zonal index*. The index is at its maximum when the air flow is clearly from west to east (1 in the diagram).

Over a period of 3 to 8 weeks, the waves grow more and more pronounced until the flow breaks into separate cells, or pockets, of rotating air. When the ridges and troughs are at their most extreme (3 in the diagram) warm air is flowing north and cold air is flowing south. This can bring extreme weather to affected areas. Then, when the index reaches its minimum (4 in the diagram) the entire system often becomes stationary for several weeks. Until the zonal flow reestablishes itself, in lower latitudes the weather remains dominated by low-pressure regions and in high latitudes by high-pressure regions. This is called *blocking*.

Figure 6: *The index cycle.*

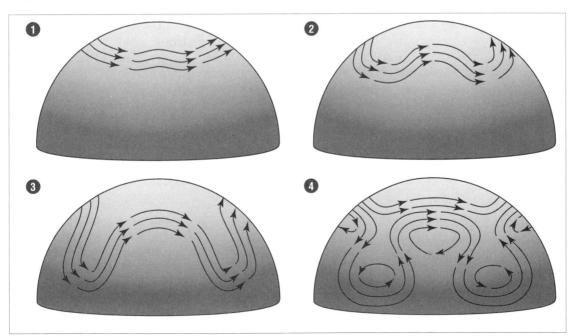

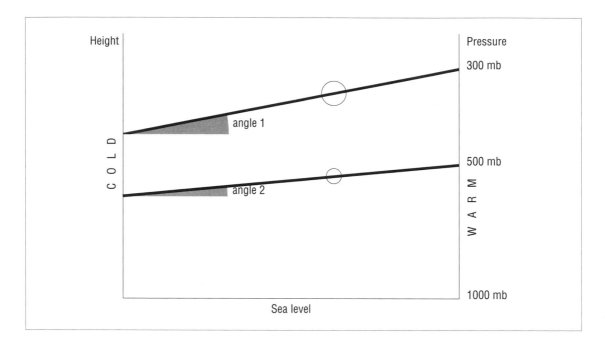

Figure 7: *Thermal winds.*

Winds blow because a pressure gradient exists and above the surface they blow at right angles to the pressure gradient (see page 10). The jet stream is also produced by a pressure gradient, but it is known as a "thermal wind."

Weather maps join together places where the atmospheric pressure is the same. The lines they use are called *isobars*. The distance between isobars indicates the steepness of the pressure gradient. If, for example, the surface pressure falls from 1,000 millibars (mb) to 800 mb over a distance of 100 miles, the gradient is steeper than it would be if pressure fell by the same amount over a distance of 200 miles and the isobars will be closer together, like the elevation contours marking steep and gentle slopes on an ordinary map. This also means the wind will be stronger, because the steeper the gradient the harder it blows.

Pressure also decreases with height and so it is possible to draw a vertical cross section of part of the atmosphere, with isobars linking altitudes where the pressure is the same. Figure 7 is a drawing of this kind, showing three isobars, for 1,000 mb (sea level), 500 mb, and 300 mb. As you see, the isobars are not horizontal. Both slope and the upper one slopes more steeply than the lower one (angle 1 is greater than angle 2). If the diagram showed all the intermediate isobars, it would be clear that the angle of slope increases steadily with height.

The sloping isobars also mark the boundaries of layers in which the air pressure is the same and the layer shown is thicker on the right of the diagram than on the left. The thickness of the layers is

George Hadley and Hadley cells

When European ships began venturing far from their home ports, into the tropics and across the equator, sailors learned that the trade winds are very dependable in both strength and direction. They made use of them, and by the end of the 16th century their existence was well known.

Many years passed, however, before anyone know why the trade winds blow so reliably. Like many scientific explanations, this one developed in stages.

Edmund Halley (1656–1742), the English astronomer, was the first person to offer an explanation. In 1686 he suggested that air at the equator is heated more strongly than air anywhere else. The warm equatorial air rises, cold air flows in near the surface from either side to replace it, and this inflowing air forms the trade winds. If this were so, however, the trades either side of the equator would flow from due north and south. In fact, they flow from the northeast and southeast.

There the matter rested until 1735. In that year George Hadley (1685–1768), an English meteorologist, proposed a modification of the Halley theory. Hadley agreed that warm equatorial air rises and is replaced at the surface, but said that the rotation of the Earth from west to east swings the moving air, making the winds blow from the northeast and south-east.

Hadley was right about what happened, but not about the reason for it. This was discovered in 1856 by the American meteorologist William Ferrel (1817–91), who said the swing is due to the tendency of moving air to rotate about its own axis, like coffee stirred in a cup.

In accounting for the trade winds, Hadley had proposed a general explanation for the

Three-cell model of atmospheric circulation.

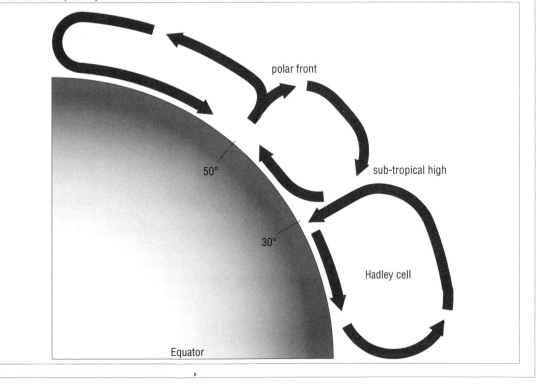

polar front

sub-tropical high

50°

30°

Hadley cell

Equator

way heat is transported away from the equator. He suggested that the warm equatorial air moves at a great height all the way to the poles, where it descends. When this kind of vertical movement occurs driven by heating from below, in a fluid, it is called a *convection cell*; the cell Hadley described is known as a *Hadley cell*.

The rotation of the Earth prevents a single, huge Hadley cell from forming. What really happens is more complicated. In various equatorial regions, warm air rises to a height of about 10 miles, moves away from the equator, cools, and descends between latitudes 25° and 30° N and S. These are the Hadley cells. When it reaches the surface in the tropics, some of the air flows back toward the equator and some flows away from the equator.

Over the poles, cold air descends and flows away from the poles at a low level. At about latitude 50° it meets air flowing away from the equatorial Hadley cells. Where the two types of air meet is called the *Polar Front*. Air rises again at the Polar Front. Some flows toward the pole, completing a high-latitude cell, and some flows toward the equator until it meets the descending air of the Hadley cell, which it joins.

There are three sets of cells in each hemisphere. This is called the *three-cell model* of atmospheric circulation by which warm air moves away from the equator and cool air moves toward the equator.

proportional to the temperature of the air in them. In cold air the layers are thinner than they are in warm air. On the left of the diagram the air is cold, and on the right it is warm.

Wind speed is proportional to the pressure gradient, so the geostrophic wind blows parallel to isobars drawn across a horizontal surface, but the changing thickness of the layers at different heights is also a gradient. This, too, produces a wind. Usually it blows in a different direction from the geostrophic wind, so the actual wind is a combination of the two. Because the thickness of the layers is proportional to temperature, it is called a *thermal wind*. It blows parallel to the layers. In the diagram this direction is at right angles to the page, so the wind at each level is shown as a circle. The strength of the thermal wind is proportional to the angle of slope (or gradient), so in the diagram the upper wind is stronger than the lower wind (indicated by the larger circle), because the upper slope is steeper than the lower one.

Thermal winds blow only where the air temperature changes over a horizontal distance. Air to one side must be cooler than air to the other side. Where this happens, the thermal wind in the northern hemisphere blows with the cool air to its left. A boundary between cool and warm air is a front and the front responsible for the strongest of all thermal winds, the Polar Front Jet Stream, is called the Polar Front.

It results from the way warm air moves by convection between the equator and poles, a circulation developed from the one first suggested in 1735 by the English meteorologist George Hadley (see box on page 21). Hadley wanted to explain why the trade winds blow so reliably in the tropics from an easterly direction, so his interest was in tropical weather. He suggested that warm air rises over the equator, moves north and south away from the equator at a high level, then descends over the poles and flows back, toward the equator, at low level.

This is not what really happens, but it is close. Very cold, dense air does sink over the poles. It then moves away from the poles at low level until it meets low-level warmer air moving toward the poles. In the northern hemisphere this meeting takes place at about 50° N, although the latitude varies from place to place and with the seasons. In winter, it is a little north of 30° N over the United States, passing across Texas, Louisiana, Alabama, and Georgia. It moves farther north as it crosses the Atlantic and runs along the English Channel at about 50° N. In summer it moves north to about 37° over the United States and about 51° over Britain. It crosses the Pacific in about the same latitudes, but is farther north over Asia. A similar meeting takes place in the southern hemisphere.

It is in these latitudes that polar air moving in one direction meets tropical air moving in the opposite direction. This meeting forms the Polar Front. Figure 8 is a simple diagram showing how this happens.

Figure 8: *The Polar Front Jet Stream.*

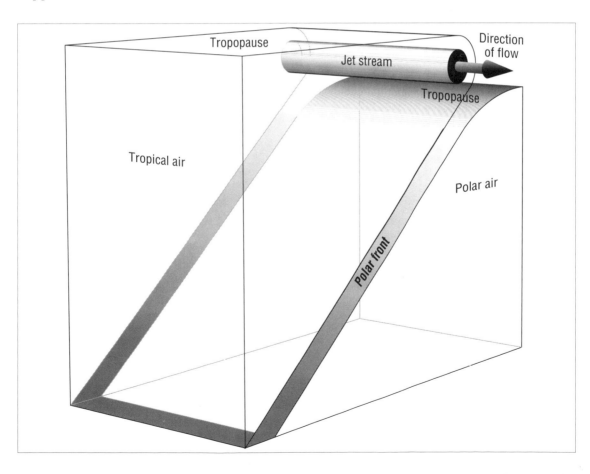

Obviously, there is a big difference in temperature between the two types of air. This gives rise to high-level thermal winds. They blow with the cold air to their left in the northern hemisphere and to their right in the southern hemisphere, so in both cases the winds blow from west to east (they are westerlies).

The strength of the upper-air westerlies is proportional to the thickness of the pressure layers in the atmosphere. This increases with height and so the wind speed increases with altitude until, at around 30,000 feet, they reach their greatest strength in the Polar Front Jet Stream.

Squall lines

Shenandoah was the pride of the U.S. Navy. Built in Philadelphia and assembled at Lakehurst, N.J., work on it started in 1919 and was completed in 1923, the year of its maiden flight. *Shenandoah* was an airship, and in those days most people believed airships were the flying machines of the future. Its design was based on that of one of the German zeppelins but avoided some of its dangers. In particular, its lift was provided by helium rather than hydrogen. It was its 7 million cubic feet of hydrogen that was to cause the *Hindenburg* airship to burst into flames spectacularly at Lakehurst in 1937. Helium is rare and costs much more than hydrogen, but it does not burn. *Shenandoah* was hailed as a very safe ship.

Following its first flight, *Shenandoah* made a trip all the way across the United States and back, a total of 9,000 miles that took it 235 hours. It made many other journeys, mainly so the Navy could show it off to the public. The airship, nearly 700 feet long, nearly 80 feet wide, and powered by six 300-horsepower engines, was an impressive sight.

A little before 3 P.M. on September 2, 1925, *Shenandoah* cast off from its mooring masts at Lakehurst, bound for Detroit on its 57th flight. The ship sailed westward into the evening and through the night, but early the next morning, before dawn, the captain noticed lightning to the north and east. *Shenandoah* turned south, away from the storm, only to be confronted by a bank of fast-moving cloud. There was no time to take evasive action, and the airship was caught in a violent upcurrent. The crew released some of the helium to slow the ascent, but then a downcurrent sent them plunging toward the ground and they released some of the water used as ballast. It was all to no avail. Another upcurrent broke the airship into two pieces, which then disintegrated. *Shenandoah* crashed in eastern Ohio. It was not a single, isolated thunderstorm that destroyed it, but something much bigger and more violent.

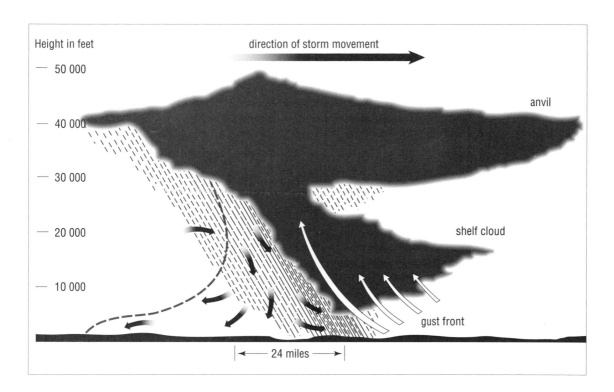

Figure 9: *Squall line storm.*

Shenandoah had flown directly into a squall line. A *squall* is a short-lived but violent storm in which the wind speed increases by at least 30 MPH. As its name suggests, a *squall line* or *line squall* is a line of storms, usually thunderstorms, several miles thick, more than 30,000 feet tall, and sometimes hundreds of miles long, but with gaps between clusters of storms. A squall line moves, as a line of storms, at speeds of 30 MPH or more. One crossed southern England in 1959 traveling at about 44 MPH.

In middle latitudes, over North America and Europe, most squall lines move from west to east or northwest to southeast. In the tropics they tend to travel in an easterly direction. This is because they move with the prevailing winds, which are westerly in middle latitudes and easterly in the tropics.

High-level cloud often provides the first advance warning of an approaching line squall. This is the *anvil*, blown ahead of the main cloud by the high-level wind. Cloud covers much of the sky, thinly at first but quickly thickening and becoming lower. It may not be possible to distinguish them from below, but a second layer of cloud appears below the high-level anvil. This is the *shelf cloud*. Rain falls from the high-level cloud into the shelf cloud, but this rain does not reach the ground. Ragged fragments of cloud drift below the main mass of cloud, but if it is possible to see beyond them, in the distance there will be what looks like a solid wall of cloud reaching almost

Adiabatic warming and cooling

Air is compressed by the weight of air above it. Imagine a balloon partly inflated with air and made from some substance that totally insulates the air inside. No matter what the temperature outside the balloon, the temperature of the air inside remains the same.

Imagine the balloon is released into the atmosphere. The air inside is squeezed between the weight of air above it, all the way to the top of the atmosphere, and the denser air below it.

Suppose the air inside the balloon is less dense than the air above it. The balloon will rise. As it rises, the distance to the top of the atmosphere becomes smaller, so there is less air above to weigh down on the air in the balloon. At the same time, as it moves through air that is less dense, it experiences less pressure from below. This causes the air in the balloon to expand.

When air (or any gas) expands, its molecules move farther apart. The *amount* of air remains the same, but it occupies a bigger volume. As they move apart, the molecules must "push" other molecules out of their way. This uses energy, so as the air expands its molecules lose energy. Because they have less energy they move more slowly.

When a moving moving molecule strikes something, some of its energy of motion (kinetic energy) is transferred to whatever it strikes and part of that energy is converted into heat. This raises the temperature of the struck object by an amount related to the number of molecules striking it and their speed.

In expanding air, the molecules are moving farther apart, so a smaller number of them strike an object each second. They are also traveling more slowly, so they strike with less force. This means the temperature of the air decreases. As it expands, air cools.

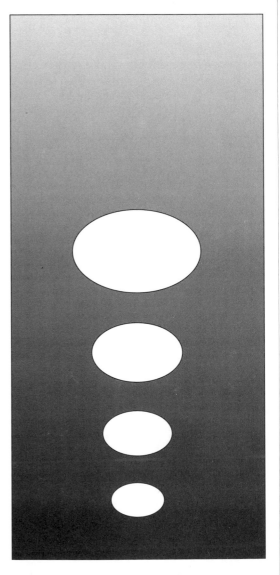

Effect of air pressure on rising and sinking air: Air is compressed by the weight of air above it. A "parcel" or "bubble" of air is squeezed between the weight of air above the denser air below. As it rises into a region of less dense air it expands. As it sinks into denser air it contracts.

to the ground. Its base may be parallel to the ground, or shaped like an arch. Then the wind will change direction, strengthen, and become gusty at a *gust front* where air is being drawn into and spilling from the base of the storm. Wind speeds in a severe squall can reach 100 MPH, with even stronger gusts. The temperature will drop rapidly, often by 10° F a minute or more, and the air pressure will suddenly rise. After that the rain will start in the region behind the main cloud mass where air is descending. The heaviest fall will come first and may be accompanied or preceded by hail. There will probably be thunder and lightning. Figure 9 shows a cross section of how a squall line storm might appear to someone watching it pass from a safe distance.

Squall lines also generate tornadoes. On May 2 and 3, 1956, a squall line crossing the United States triggered about 30 tornadoes, and the 148 tornadoes of the "Super Outbreak" on April 3 and 4, 1974, were produced by three separate squall lines that all developed at the same time. Between them, these squall lines extended from the southern shores of Lake Michigan to central Alabama.

For a squall line to occur, two air masses with different characteristics must collide. Most commonly it is cold air that collides with warm air, but sometimes it is a collision between dry and moist air. In either case, there must also be wind shear at high level. *Wind shear* is a strong wind blowing in a direction other than that of the lower winds. This is needed to carry away rising air.

Most squall lines begin when a mass of cold, dry, dense air moves forward very fast against a mass of warm, moist, less dense air. This produces a cold front, but a very vigorous one, due to its speed. The dense air pushes beneath the less dense air, forcing it to rise. As it rises, the pressure acting on the air from above decreases, because it is the weight of the overlying air that exerts the pressure and the greater the altitude the smaller the amount of air above. With the pressure reduced, the air expands and when air expands it cools. This cooling is due only to expansion and has nothing to do with the temperature of the surrounding air. It is called *adiabatic* cooling (see box on page 26).

Warm air can hold more water vapor than cold air, so when air cools its water vapor starts to condense into liquid droplets. Clouds form (see box on page 32). Condensation releases heat, however, and this warms the surrounding air, making it rise farther and cool again, causing more water vapor to condense. The clouds grow bigger and bigger.

In a squall line, the wind above the clouds blows from a different direction to the wind lower down, carrying away the rising air. This is called *divergence* and it produces a region of low atmospheric pressure in the lower part of the clouds. Air at ground level is drawn into the low-pressure area and immediately rises, feeding the cloud

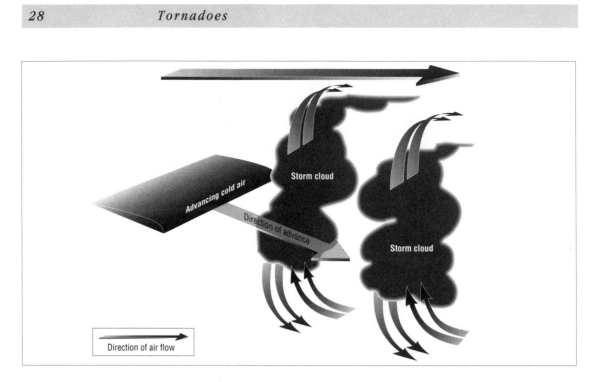

Figure 10: *Squall line.*

with air and moisture. Elsewhere in the clouds, air that has risen nearly to the top and has been chilled by its rise contracts into a smaller volume, becomes denser than the air above and around it and sinks again without leaving the cloud top. There are then two sets of air currents inside and beneath the cloud, one entering the cloud and rising, the other sinking from the cloud and leaving. Figure 10 illustrates what happens. While all this is happening, the dense air is still advancing, churning up the air ahead of it and pushing it into the upcurrents.

At this stage the squall line earns its name. By now the clouds have become storm clouds, called *cumulonimbus*, and they tower to a great height. Then, for reasons scientists do not really understand, they form groups along a line and the strong, gusting wind at their leading edges, where air is being drawn into the low-pressure region, becomes continuous over long distances. This is the squall line itself, the narrow belt of strong, blustery winds.

During the early stages of its development, the cold downcurrents in the cloud meet the updrafts and start to slow them. Cold, descending air starts to spread horizontally, but the rising air flows over its edge and forms a new upcurrent to the side. After a time this, too, meets its own spreading downcurrent, flows around its edge, and becomes a new current. Eventually, the upcurrents and downcurrents separate completely. Upcurrents draw in air ahead of the line, downcurrents sink to the rear of the line, but the sinking air then diverges, some of it flowing forward beneath the upcurrents and out of the front of the line. Rain is associated with the downcurrents, which is why the rain and hail fall at the rear of the cloud mass.

The stream of cold, sinking air that flows beneath the less dense air ahead of the storm line forces more air to rise and new clouds to form. As they form, downcurrents from the new clouds produce still more clouds ahead of them. This movement, which triggers the formation of new cloud, is also what produces the strong gustiness of the wind.

Not even huge storm clouds last for more than a few hours, but those in a squall line constantly regenerate themselves. They do so at first by producing new upcurrents to the side of their own downcurrents and later by triggering new cloud formation in front of themselves. As the line advances it looks like a solid mass of clouds all moving together. In fact, old clouds are constantly disappearing at the rear of the line and new ones forming at the front. This is how the line moves.

The storm system is now perpetuating itself. An advancing mass of dense air started the process, but now it can continue independently. The storm line starts to move faster than the air mass behind it. If it lasts long enough, the squall line can move hundreds of miles ahead of the cold front.

It can happen that the collision triggering the formation of a squall line is between dry and moist air, both at much the same temperature. When this happens, the dry air may flow over the top of the moist air, trapping it beneath. This will cause clouds to form as moist air rises through the overlying dry air. The effect is usually fairly mild, but if the moist air is already cloudy, cumulus and then cumulonimbus clouds will develop (see "cloud classification" in volume 6). Alternatively, if the dry air flows beneath the moist air, the moist air will be forced upward and the effect will be the same as that produced by a cold front.

Squall lines advance because individual storm clouds are feeding one another. This mechanism also makes it possible for squall lines to develop even when there is no front to trigger them.

This development begins with a single, huge storm cloud. Within the cloud, upcurrents of warm air conflict with the downcurrents of cold air bringing the rain and hail. If the cloud is big enough, the currents tend to separate, so warm air is being drawn into one region of the cloud and cold air is sinking and moving away from another area. The sinking air may then flow beneath the warmer surrounding air, just as it does ahead of a squall line and with similar results. One cloud supplies cold air at ground level to lift warmer air and start it cooling. In effect, the outflow of air creates a kind of artificial cold front, with each storm cloud triggering the formation of others along it. Once formed, this type of squall line behaves in exactly the same way as one triggered by a real cold front.

Storms can also merge into one another if several form independently but fairly close together. Again, no cold front is needed to start them growing, because they can begin as ordinary thunderstorms (see below). When they merge, however, they may align themselves and grow into a squall line.

Cold fronts are by far the commonest trigger, however, and the most vigorous cold fronts occur where tropical and polar air meet. This most often happens close to the Polar Front and it is at the Polar Front that the jet stream provides a strong wind shear to start squall lines forming. These most often occur in spring, which is when the Polar Front and its jet stream are moving north across North America (see figures 5A and 5B on pages 17–18).

Tornadoes linked to squall-line storms can be very violent indeed, but squall lines are only one source of tornadoes. Isolated thunderstorms can also produce them, and much less predictably.

Thunderstorms

All tornadoes are triggered by thunderstorms, but only the very biggest thunderstorms trigger tornadoes. Thunderstorms begin when unstable air rises. To be "unstable," a deep layer of air must be less dense than the air immediately above it. Being less dense, it rises through the air above it and goes on rising until it lies beneath air less dense than itself and can rise no higher.

Its rise may begin when, in a particular location, the ground is warmed strongly by the Sun. The warmed air expands and this makes it less dense than the air above it, so it rises. That is how summer storms begin. Alternatively, moving air may be forced to rise as it crosses hills or mountains and warm air may be lifted by denser air at an advancing cold front.

Just because air is forced to rise, it does not follow that a thunderstorm will develop or, indeed, that clouds of any kind will form. If stable air is made to rise it will reach a level beyond which it can rise no higher, then sink again. As it rises it cools adiabatically and as it sinks it warms adiabatically (see box on page 26).

Whether or not air is unstable, and continues rising, depends on the difference between its rate of adiabatic cooling and that at which the temperature of the surrounding air decreases with height. Air temperature always decreases with height, but not everywhere at the same rate. Suppose, for example, that when the temperature at sea level in a particular place was +50° F the temperature 10,000 feet above that place was -10° F. That would amount to a drop of 60° F over 10,000 feet, or 6° F for every 1,000 feet. In this example, 6° F per 1,000 feet is the rate of temperature decrease (or lapse) that is actually measured. It is called the *environmental lapse rate*, or ELR.

Rising air cools at the *dry adiabatic lapse rate*, or DALR (see box on page 32) of 5.5° F per 1,000 feet, so if air in that place is forced to rise, it will cool more slowly than the rate at which the temperature of the surrounding air decreases with height. The ELR is greater than the DALR, so, as it rises, the air will always be just slightly warmer than the air immediately above it. It will be less dense, and, therefore, it will go on rising until it reaches a level where the two lapse rates are the same.

Air is unstable if the ELR exceeds the DALR. If the situation is reversed and the DALR exceeds the ELR, rising air will cool faster than the rate at which the temperature of the surrounding air decreases with height. This will prevent it from rising, because as soon as it does so it becomes cooler and denser than the air around and above it. This air is stable and if it is forced to rise, as soon as the force ceases it will sink again.

Unless the air is extremely dry, however, the rate of adiabatic cooling will change long before the air has cooled to -10° F, because the water vapor it contains will have started to condense into droplets. Warm water can hold more water vapor than cold air, so as the air cools it must rid itself of its excess water vapor. The temperature at which condensation begins is called the *dew-point temperature*. It varies according to the amount of water vapor present in the air, or, to put it another way, the more water vapor the air contains, the closer it is to being saturated. You can use experiment 11 in volume 6 to measure the dew-point temperature.

The height at which rising air cools to its dew-point temperature and water vapor condenses into liquid droplets is called the *lifting condensation level*. It is the height of the cloud base. The height at which air stops rising marks the cloud top.

When water vapor condenses, it releases heat, called the *latent heat* of condensation. This warms the air around it and if the air is still rising it slows the rate at which it cools adiabatically from the DALR to the *saturated adiabatic lapse rate,* or SALR. The SALR varies, but it averages about 3° F per 1,000 feet.

If the air is unstable, meaning the ELR is greater than the DALR, condensation will increase its instability, because the difference between the ELR and the SALR is even greater than that between the ELR and the DALR. So the air will continue rising. It is still cooling, so its water vapor will continue to condense, releasing latent heat and maintaining the SALR. When the air temperature falls below freezing, the water vapor will form tiny ice crystals instead of water. This releases even more latent heat (see box on page 34).

Eventually the rising air reaches a ceiling. By then it is very cold. It is also dry because almost all its water vapor has condensed. Warmer air, rising from below, disturbs it and it starts to sink. As it descends it begins to warm adiabatically, but, because it is dry, it warms at the DALR, so it is warming faster than the rising air is

Evaporation, condensation, and the formation of clouds

When air rises it cools adiabatically, by an average of 5.5° F every 1,000 feet. This is called the *dry adiabatic lapse rate*. Moving air may be forced to rise if it crosses high ground, such as a mountain or mountain range, or meets a mass of cooler, denser air at a front. Locally, air may also rise by convection where the ground is warmed unevenly.

There will be a height, called the *lifting condensation level*, at which its temperature falls to its dew point. As the air rises above this level the water vapor it contains will start to condense. Condensation releases latent heat, warming the air. After the relative humidity of the air reaches 100% and the air continues to rise, it will cool at the saturated adiabatic lapse rate of about 3° F per 1,000 feet.

Cloud formation.

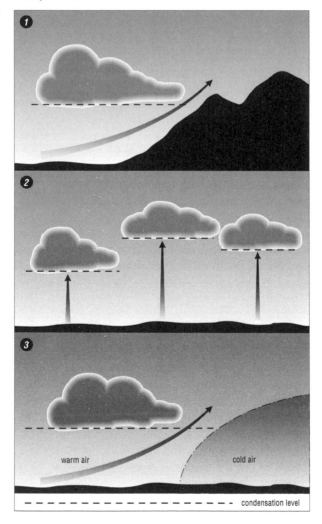

warm air   cold air

– condensation level

Water vapor will condense at a relative humidity as low as 78% if the air contains minute particles of a substance that readily dissolves in water. Salt crystals and sulfate particles are common examples. If the air contains insoluble particles, such as dust, the vapor will condense at about 100% relative humidity. If there are no particles at all, the relative humidity may exceed 100% and the air will be supersaturated, although the relative humidity in clouds rarely exceeds 101%.

The particles onto which water vapor condenses are called *cloud condensation nuclei* (CCN). They range in size from 0.001 μm to more than 10 μm in diameter; water will condense onto the smallest particles only if the air is strongly supersaturated and the largest particles are so heavy they do not remain airborne very long. Condensation is most efficient on CCN averaging 0.2 μm diameter (1 μm = one-millionth of a meter = 0.00004 inches).

At first, water droplets vary in size according to the size of the nuclei onto which they condensed. After that, the droplets grow but also lose water by evaporation because they are warmed by the latent heat of condensation. Some freeze, grow into snowflakes, and then melt as they fall into a lower, warmer region of the cloud. Others grow as large droplets collide and merge with smaller ones.

cooling (at the SALR). There are now currents of rising air and currents of sinking air. In a big, towering cloud the upcurrents may be moving at more than 60 MPH, the downcurrents more slowly. As the temperature of the sinking air reaches the dew-point temperature water droplets evaporate into it. Evaporation absorbs latent heat, which cools the air.

Because of these swirling upcurrents and downcurrents, clouds that form in unstable air have heaped shapes, like cotton wool or cauliflower. Such clouds are called *cumulus*. As they grow wider and taller they become *cumulonimbus*. Cumulonimbus clouds produce rain showers, which are often heavy.

A cumulonimbus cloud, formed in very unstable air, is large and quite complex. In its lower levels there are liquid water droplets. Some of these collide with one another and merge, to form larger droplets. Those that grow too heavy to remain airborne fall as rain.

Near the top of the cloud, there are ice crystals. High-level winds may draw these out into long streamers, shaped rather like a blacksmith's anvil. The anvil ends where the ice crystals are drawn into air dry enough for them to change directly (sublime) into invisible water vapor. They fall as they are drawn out, but once clear of the main cloud they enter dry air and turn into water vapor. This makes the ice-crystal stream taper, with the thicker end close to the cloud top, and that is what gives the cloud its anvil shape. Thunder was once believed to the sound of the god Thor beating with a hammer on this anvil.

Some of the ice crystals link together and form snowflakes. The bigger snowflakes are too heavy to remain at the top of the cloud, so they fall, forming a layer of snowflakes in the middle of the cloud.

Latent heat and dew point

Water can exist in three different states, or phases: gas (water vapor), liquid (water), or solid (ice). In the gaseous phase, molecules are free to move in all directions. In the liquid phase, molecules join together in short "strings." In the solid phase, molecules form a closed structure with a space at the center. As water cools, its molecules move closer together and the liquid becomes denser. Pure water at sea-level pressure reaches its densest at 39° F. Below this temperature, the molecules start forming ice crystals. Because these have a space at the center, ice is less dense than water and, weight for weight, has a greater volume. That is why water expands when it freezes and why ice floats on the surface of water.

Molecules bond to one another in the liquid and solid states by the attraction of opposite charges, and energy must be supplied to break those bonds. This energy is absorbed by the molecules without changing their temperature and the same amount of energy is released when the bonds form again. This is called *latent heat*. For pure water, 600 calories of energy are absorbed to change one gram (1 g = 0.035 oz.) from liquid to gas (evaporation) and 80 calories to melt one gram of ice. Sublimation, the direct change from ice to vapor without passing through the liquid phase, absorbs 680 calories for each gram (the sum of the latent heats of melting and evaporation). In each case, the same amount of energy is

Latent heat.

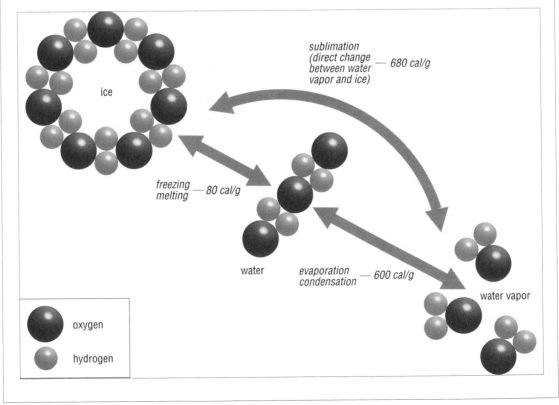

sublimation
(direct change
between water — 680 cal/g
vapor and ice)

ice

freezing — 80 cal/g
melting

water

evaporation — 600 cal/g
condensation

water vapor

oxygen

hydrogen

released when water vapor condenses into liquid water and when water freezes.

Energy to supply the latent heat is taken from the surrounding air or water. When ice melts or water evaporates, the air and water in contact with them are cooled, because energy has been taken from them. That is why it often feels cold during a thaw and why our bodies can cool themselves by sweating and allowing the sweat to evaporate.

When latent heat is released by freezing and condensation, the surroundings are warmed. This is very important in the formation of the storm clouds from which hurricanes and tornadoes develop. Warm air rises, its water vapor condenses, and this warms the air still more, making it rise higher.

Warm air can hold more water vapor than cool air. If moist air is cooled, its water vapor will condense into liquid droplets. The temperature at which this occurs is called the *dew point*. It is the temperature at which dew forms on surfaces and evaporates from them.

At the dew-point temperature, the air is saturated with water vapor. The amount of moisture in the air is usually expressed as its *relative humidity*. This is the amount of water present as a percentage of the amount needed to saturate the air at that temperature.

Snowflakes which fall below this level melt and become liquid droplets. Figure 11 shows what is happening inside a cloud of this type.

Big cumulonimbus clouds often form on really warm summer days. In fact, that is when they are very likely to form. All that is needed to trigger their development is strongly warmed ground and moist air. These often occur together in summer. As you swelter in the humid heat, it may seem strange to think that there is ice in the cloud above you. If you doubt it, a shower of hail ought to convince you, but ordinary rain usually begins as ice that melts on its way down.

Small ice crystals make ideal condensation nuclei. Near the cloud top, where water vapor turns directly into ice, in addition to the crystals there are many droplets of water cooled to below freezing temperature. These freeze onto ice crystals, so the crystals grow at the expense of the supercooled droplets. When they reach a certain size, the crystals start to fall and melt as they pass through the warmer air below. If they continue downward and fall from the bottom of the cloud, they will reach the ground as rain. In cold weather, they may not pass through air warm enough to melt them, in which case they fall as snow. Snow rarely falls where the air temperature exceeds 39° F. If the temperature is very close to this, snow may fall mixed with rain. In Britain, this mixture is called *sleet*.

Only cumulonimbus clouds produce hail because these are the only clouds that contain sufficiently strong vertical currents. The life of a hailstone begins when a water droplet is carried aloft by an upcurrent, enters much colder air, and freezes. It is now a tiny ball of clear ice. Supercooled water droplets freeze onto it, covering it with rime ice. The hailstone then starts to fall. When it enters slightly warmer air at a lower level, where there are many water droplets,

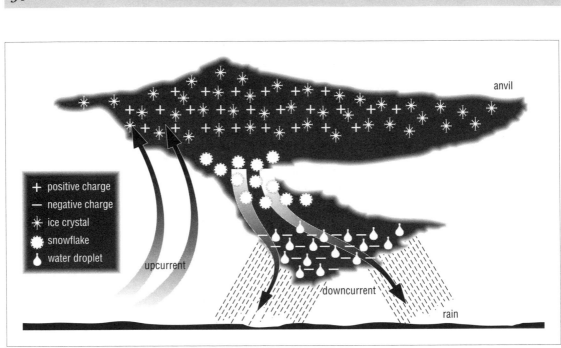

Figure 11: *Inside a storm cloud.*

more of them collect around it. The hailstone now comprises a tiny ball of clear ice, surrounded by a layer of white, rime ice, and outside that a layer of liquid water. An upcurrent now carries it aloft again, freezing the outer layer of water to form more clear ice, onto which more supercooled droplets freeze as rime ice. The hailstone continues to fall and rise in this way, on each trip collecting another layer of clear ice and another layer of rime ice, until it is too heavy to be lifted by the upcurrents. At this point it falls from the cloud, too fast for it to melt significantly. Its size is an indication of the strength of the vertical currents inside the cloud which made it. Occasionally, hailstones can reach a very large size. In 1970, at Coffeyville, Kansas, there was a hailstorm in which some of the hailstones weighed 3 pounds.

At this stage, rain or snow, and perhaps hail, are falling heavily enough for people to call it a storm. It is not yet a thunderstorm, but it is rapidly developing into one. Scientists still do not understand exactly how this begins. Several explanations have been proposed, one of which seems more likely than the others. It starts with collisions between hailstones and tiny splinters of ice.

Whether it is a solid (ice), liquid (water), or gas (water vapor), water consists of molecules in each of which two hydrogen atoms are bonded to one oxygen atom. They are not joined together in a straight line, however, but with both the hydrogens on the same side of the oxygen, separated from each other by an angle of 104.5° (see figure 12). Each oxygen atom carries a negative (-) electric charge and each hydrogen a positive (+) electric charge, so, because of the way the atoms are arranged, a water molecule has a slight negative charge at its oxygen end and a slight positive charge at its hydrogen end. Such molecules are said to be "polar."

When a supercooled water droplet freezes, it does so from the outside in and its freezing releases latent heat. This supplies energy to the water molecules. The hydrogen atoms are much smaller than the oxygen atoms and move more easily. This "injection" of energy makes them turn their molecules around, so the negative end points toward the center of the droplet and the positive points outward. An ice crystal, descending through the cloud, collides with the frozen droplet, knocking a splinter of ice from it. This splinter, from the outside of the droplet, contains more positive than negative charge, and when it breaks away it leaves the rest of the droplet with more negative than positive charge. The ice splinter is very small and light. It is carried upward by a rising air current. The frozen droplet is bigger and sinks to a low level inside the cloud.

The effect is tiny, but there are countless millions of collisions. Little by little, positively charged splinters of ice accumulate high in the cloud and negatively charged droplets accumulate lower down.

Whether or not this is really the way it happens, or all that happens, there is no doubt that the upper part of the cloud comes to carry a positive electric charge and the lower part a negative one. The negative charge near the cloud base may then induce a positive charge on the ground below it.

Air is a good electric insulator, so these separated charges cannot equalize themselves by a flow of current from the positive to the

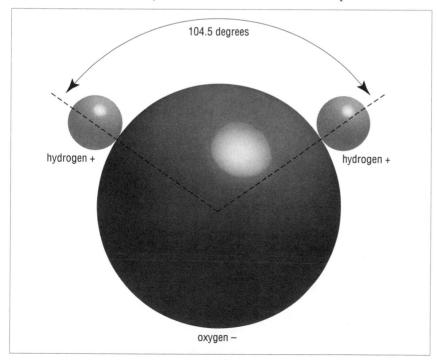

Figure 12: *The water molecule.*

104.5 degrees

hydrogen +   hydrogen +

oxygen −

Figure 13: *Lightning.*
(NASA)

negative regions. The charges continue to accumulate until there are places where the strength of the electric field inside the cloud, and between the cloud base and the ground, is enough to trigger a huge spark, flashing from positive to negative and neutralizing the charge.

What we see as lightning is this electric spark. It may flash from one part of the cloud to another, in which case we see it as "sheet" lightning, a bright flash with no visible center. It may flash from one cloud to another. Or it may flash between a cloud and the ground, as a "fork" of lightning. Electricity flows from positive to negative, of course, and forked lightning comprises two flashes following one another so closely they look like a single flash, lasting about one-fifth of a second. The first flash is from the (positive) ground to the (negative) cloud base. The spark follows a line of least resistance among the air molecules. This makes it jump from side to side and gives the fork its jagged shape. As it moves, the spark releases so much energy that it knocks molecules apart, leaving an invisible line through the air in which the air itself is electrically charged. The flow of current is so large that for an instant it reverses the charges. The cloud base becomes positively charged, the ground negatively charged, and a second spark flashes from the cloud to the ground following the path already made by the first spark. This second spark is the one we see.

Energy released by the lightning flash heats the air along its path. Heating causes the air to expand, but it is so intense and so sudden there is no time for the surrounding air to move aside for it. Quite literally, the air explodes, sending out the shock waves we hear as thunder.

How a tornado begins

Isolated thunderstorms that generate tornadoes are called *tornadic* storms. Their appearance is a little different from that of squall-line storms (see page 24), but they produce similar effects.

When you are beneath a big cloud it is almost impossible to estimate the height of its base, or in the case of a cumulonimbus, its bases, for it extends to the side in what look like shelves. One of those shelves, joining the really huge tower of a tornadic storm cloud at a quite low level, may be the inner edge of the anvil. The rest of the anvil, its base sloping upward, stretches away from the tower for several miles. If you are standing directly in the path of the approaching cloud and facing it, in the northern hemisphere its anvil will stretch toward you and to your right (see figure 14). In the southern hemisphere it will stretch to the left.

On the lowest part of the anvil base there may be a quite unmistakable feature. Many smooth, udder-shaped clouds may look as though they are suspended from the base of the main cloud. This type of cloud is called *mammatus*, from the Old English version of

Figure 14: *Direction of movement and location of anvil in a tornadic storm.*

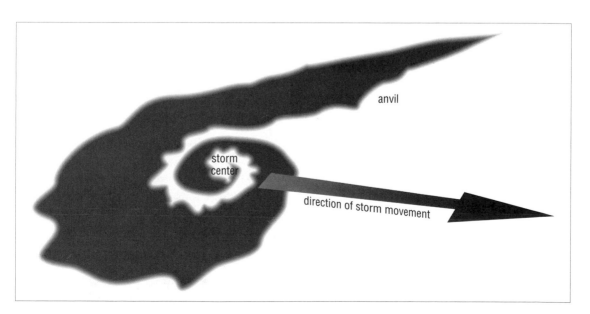

Figure 15 A: *The development of a tornado.* (National Center for Atmospheric Research, Boulder, CO)

the Latin word for breast. Mammatus probably forms as ice crystals in the anvil sublime (change directly from ice to water vapor without passing through a liquid phase) into the dry air above them. Sublimation absorbs a large amount of latent heat, so it sharply cools small pools of surrounding air. Their density increases, so they sink just far enough to produce the mammatus effect.

Mammatus can form only where the anvil is very large, and very large anvils indicate very violent upcurrents and a layer of stable air above the cloud. Rising air cannot penetrate the stable layer, so it spills sideways. This is what forms the anvil, and the size of the anvil is a measure of the amount of water vapor the upcurrents feed into it. The bigger it is, the more water it contains, and so the more vigorous the upcurrents must be.

Violent upcurrents are necessary for the formation of tornadoes, so the appearance of mammatus beneath an approaching cloud is a clear warning. It does not mean tornadoes are present, but it does mean they are possible or even likely.

Squall-line storm clouds rarely produce mammatus. With them the early warning sign is the appearance of fragments of cloud moving in a circle beneath the main cloud.

Ordinary cumulonimbus, of the kind that produces heavy showers and sometimes thunderstorms, is not tornadic. Within it, the upcurrents and downcurrents are in the same place, so they compete. While the storm lasts you feel the downcurrents as gusts of cold wind, and the combination of air entering and leaving the base of the cloud makes the wind strong and variable in direction, but eventually the downcurrents overpower the upcurrents and choke them. When that happens the storm starts to die. The main part of the cloud falls as rain or snow, with smaller drops or flakes than fell earlier, and after a few minutes nothing may remain of the cloud except for its anvil, drifting off by itself.

Where the upcurrents are strong enough to feed a really big anvil, however, the sweep of air into the anvil bends over the upper part of the upcurrents (see figure 16), carrying them clear of the downcurrents. This allows the upcurrents and downcurrents to separate, with the upcurrents overhanging the downcurrents. Rain and snow no longer fall into the upcurrents, but into the downcurrents. By this mechanism an isolated storm can become a tornadic storm. Upcurrents and downcurrents also separate in squall-line storms, but the mechanism is different (see page 28).

Even at this stage tornadoes are not inevitable. A third factor is needed to set the entire system spinning on its axis. That factor is

Figure 15 B: *The development of a tornado.*

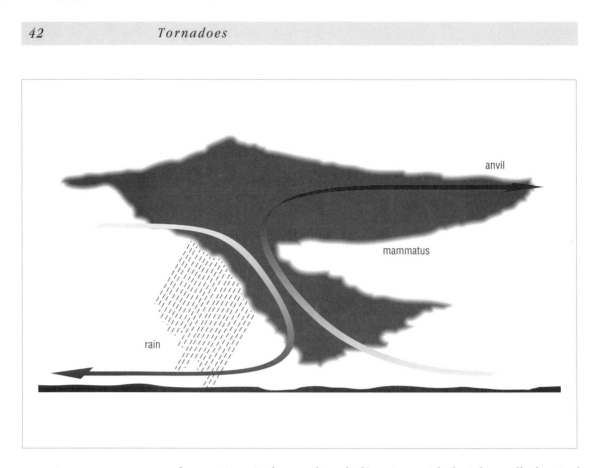

anvil

mammatus

rain

Figure 16: *Upcurrents and downcurrents in a tornadic storm.*

a change in wind speed and direction with height, called *wind shear.*

There is usually some wind shear. Because of friction, surface winds over land are always weaker than winds a few hundred feet above the ground and their direction is less constant (see page 10). In itself, this is not enough to provide the necessary amount of wind shear, but if the storm cloud lies beneath the jet stream (see page 16) or across a weather front, the high-level wind will be quite different from the wind at lower levels. The jet stream is certainly strong enough to provide considerable wind shear and frontal winds.

Upcurrents, rising through the cloud, flow in the direction of the wind. As they rise, they encounter wind from a different direction, which deflects them. Moving air tends to rotate about an axis (see page 49) and this deflection either starts the upcurrents rotating or intensifies their rotation if they are already spiraling upward.

At this stage, small wind eddies may lift dust from the ground, raising it a foot or two, twisting as it goes. If you see these miniature twisters beneath an approaching storm cloud you can be sure all the necessary ingredients are assembled. They tell you that rising air in the cloud is spinning strongly. At any moment one or more tornadoes may appear.

Supercells

Warmed air rises in upcurrents and cool air sinks in downcurrents. This is what happens in a convection cell. Experiment 12 in volume 6 shows how you can easily demonstrate this for yourself, using smoke to trace the movement of warm and cool air. It is a very common phenomenon. When you heat a pan of water on the stove, convection cells usually form in it. Warmed water rises, cools at the surface, and sinks to the bottom, where it is warmed and rises again.

Inside an ordinary cumulonimbus storm cloud, the convection cells are unstable and last no more than an hour or two. The upcurrents and downcurrents interfere with one another until the downcurrents smother the upcurrents and the cold rain and snow cool the rising air. When that happens, the storm dies down and the cloud quickly starts to dissipate. If the conditions which led to the formation of the cloud remain, another storm cloud will be forming to take the place of the first even while it is dying, so a storm can last much longer and travel farther than the individual clouds that compose it.

If the upcurrents and downcurrents separate, however, so they flow in different parts of the cloud, the resulting convection cell is much more stable. A cloud in which this happens can live for many hours.

Often there is not just one convection cell, but several. Sometimes these form when adjacent cumulonimbus clouds merge. This can happen when unstable air extends to a considerable height and there is high-level wind shear.

More often, multiple convection cells develop along squall lines (see page 24). The strong downcurrent of cold air leaving a convection cell produces a very small area in which the atmospheric pressure is just a little higher than that of the surrounding air. The denser air moves beneath the less dense air, causing it to rise. The lifted air then becomes unstable. The downcurrents beside it continue to push more and more air into it, which makes the air rise with increasing intensity until there is enough of it to form the upcurrent of a new convective cell, with its own downcurrent to repeat the process. Just by looking at it you cannot tell where one cloud ends and the next begins. It looks like, and is, a single, vast cloud, but one that contains whole clusters of convection cells. When fully developed, each individual convection cell is usually about half a mile in diameter.

Some convection cells grow much larger than this. They can be up to six miles across. A cloud containing such large convection cells reaches much greater heights than an ordinary storm cloud and it lasts far longer. These very large, stable, convective cells are called *supercells* and it is in them that the upcurrents often rise at 100 MPH or more.

If they are big enough and hot enough, surface fires can cause intense convection. After the atomic bomb was dropped on Hiroshima in 1945, and also after fires that followed an earthquake in Tokyo in 1923, the strong convection triggered several tornadoes. Tornadoes also occurred around firestorms in other cities, but those caused by the Hiroshima atomic explosion led a young Japanese scientist, Tetsuya Theodore Fujita (he took his middle name in 1968), to embark on what has become a lifelong study of tornadoes. Based at the University of Chicago, he is now probably the world's leading authority on the subject and it was he who proposed, in 1957, that tornadoes might occur in clouds of a particular type, called supercells, all of which have a similar structure or "architecture."

Inside a big cumulonimbus, never mind a fully grown supercell, conditions are extremely violent and it is for good reason that aircraft will detour many miles to avoid them. In his book *Wellington, Mainstay of Bomber Command,* Peter G. Cooksley described what can happen to a plane that accidentally flies through one.

One morning in 1944, a Wellington bomber of the Royal Air Force took off from its field northwest of London on what should have been a routine training mission. At 12,000 feet the plane entered what looked to the pilot like cumulus cloud. As the crew soon discovered, however, the cumulus hid a core of vigorous cumulonimbus storm cloud, and they flew directly into it.

Bucking and swinging about wildly, the plane was bombarded with hail and sheets of rain. The pilot and copilot were strapped into their seats, but the other members of the crew found themselves floating weightless one moment as the machine dropped from beneath them, then pressed hard into their seats as it leapt upward. Equipment that was not tied down did the same. Heavy ammunition boxes floated, then crashed to the floor, and the navigator's maps and pencils rose into the air and scattered everywhere. The needle on the airspeed indicator spun crazily and then the instrument broke, all the windows suddenly went white as they were covered with rime ice, and ice started accumulating on the wings. The pilot tried to turn back out of the cloud, but his attempt to do this sent the bomber into an uncontrolled, spiraling dive. At this point he ordered the crew to prepare to bail out.

It was the dive that saved them by throwing the plane out of the bottom of the cloud, where the ice melted from the wings and blew away and the pilot was able to regain control. They had plunged 7,000 feet, most of the time with the plane completely out of control. Miraculously, none of the crew was injured and their plane, said to be one of the strongest types of aircraft ever built, sustained only minor damage.

At least one pilot has ejected inside a thunderstorm, when the engine of his jet fighter failed and the fire warning light made him fear it was burning. He ejected at 47,000 feet, fell, then was swept upward at tremendous speed, fell again, and repeated this several times before falling from the bottom of the cloud. He spent more than half an hour inside the cloud, alternately suspended from his parachute and dragged upward by it, before finally he reached the ground.

Both of these were "merely" isolated thunderstorms. A supercell storm is very much fiercer. Large storms are often severe, but supercell storms are always severe, terrifying, and usually very dangerous. They can tear the wings from any plane that is not specially strengthened to survive them and, beneath them, they can and often do generate tornadoes.

The speed with which a huge volume of air races up the main core of upcurrent, sometimes called a *mesocyclone,* produces intensely low pressure beneath the cloud. This draws in air, causing gale-force, gusting winds and at the same time feeding the flow. Air entering the cloud is already moist and as it rises and cools its water vapor condenses. It rises so fast, however, that water vapor is carried to a great height.

There is a limit to the height rising air can reach, no matter how warm it is. Air is warmed from below by contact with the land and sea surface. It is this warming that makes air rise by convection and as it rises it cools adiabatically (see box on page 26). Rising air is

Figure 17: *Structure of the atmosphere.*

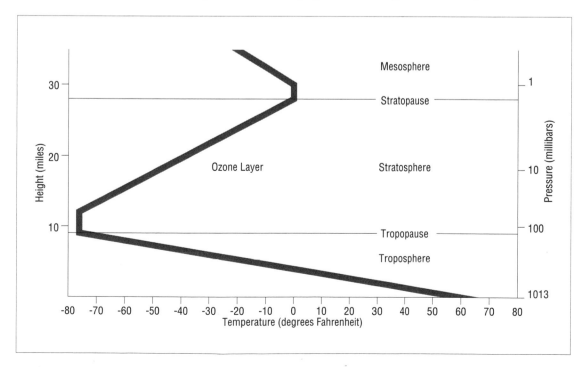

not really confined to "parcels," isolated from surrounding air. There is a great deal of mixing due to air turbulence. At the same time, latent heat released and absorbed by the condensation and evaporation of water also affect the temperature of the air in which these take place. The greater the altitude, however, the farther away the air is from the source of warming and the less affected it is by warmth carried aloft by convection. Its temperature decreases with height. The influence of latent heat also decreases with height because as the temperature continues to fall more and more water vapor is "squeezed" out of the air. Figure 17 illustrates this fall in temperature with height (the lapse rate) in a very simplified way. In fact, the lapse rate varies from place to place and from one day to the next in the same place, so the diagram shows the principle of what happens, rather than being a literal description of it.

Eventually a height is reached at which the temperature either remains constant with further increase in altitude (as shown in figure 17) or gradually increases. Ordinarily, rising air cannot rise past this height because the air above it is at the same temperature and density as itself. There is a boundary, called the *tropopause*, which divides the atmosphere into two distinct layers. In the lower layer, the *troposphere*, temperature decreases with height. In the layer above the tropopause, called the *stratosphere*, temperature is at first constant with increasing height, then increases, due mainly to the absorption of incoming solar ultraviolet radiation by oxygen and ozone. It is this absorption that forms the ozone layer. The stratosphere, too, ends with a boundary called the *stratopause*, above which, in the *mesosphere*, temperature once more decreases with height.

The name *troposphere* is from the Greek word *tropos*, which means "turning." This is the region of the atmosphere in which air rises and descends vertically. It "turns over." This is the part of the atmosphere in which almost all clouds form (a few special kinds of cloud occasionally form in the stratosphere) and weather happens. Because air is easily compressed, the weight of the overlying atmosphere presses down so much that 84% of the air making up the entire atmosphere lies below a height of 8 miles, and 94% of it lies below 18 miles. Atmospheric water vapor is confined almost wholly to the troposphere. Air in the stratosphere is very dry. The *strato* in *stratosphere* is from a Latin word meaning "strewn about," or "laid down." In the stratosphere there is very little vertical movement of air.

The height of the tropopause varies, but on average it is at about 10 miles over the equator and 5 miles over the poles. The difference is due to the much greater surface heating and resulting convection over the equator.

In a supercell cloud, the upcurrents rise so fast, with so much energy, that they overshoot the tropopause, sometimes by as much as 2 miles, with ice-crystal cloud still forming, in air with an average

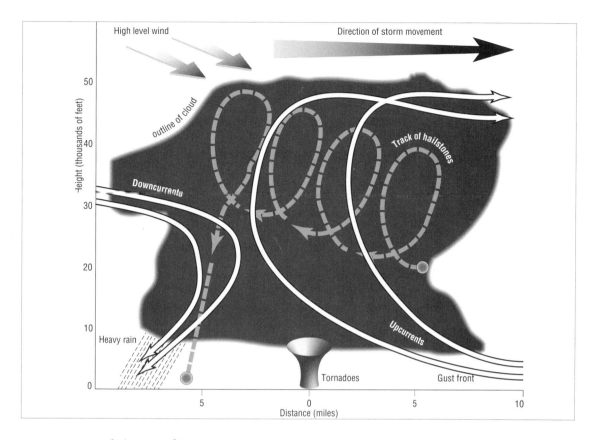

Figure 18: *Structure of a supercell.*

temperature of about -76° F. Not even a supercell can reach higher than this. Its upward motion checked, the rising air steadies, then sinks to just below the tropopause as its clouds spread downwind to form the upper part of the anvil. Seen from an aircraft flying in the stratosphere, the top of the storm cloud has a clearly marked "hump."

The supercell downcurrent is also very strong. It originates at about mid-height, as shown in figure 18, and loses none of its speed as it leaves the base of the cloud. Downcurrents are not tornadoes, but they can emerge as 75-MPH winds. Technically, this is a hurricane-force wind and it can do considerable damage, especially to farm crops. Combined with the torrential rain accompanying it, the downdraft can flatten crops on the ground (farmers call this *lodging*), leaving them soaked and almost impossible to harvest.

Hail, too, can cause severe crop damage. Hailstones begin to form in the upcurrent and grow by repeated freezing and partial melting (see page 35). As they rise and fall, they move toward the rear of the cloud, eventually falling in the downcurrent. Its fall commences when the weight of a hailstone is greater than the updraft can lift, so the size it can attain is directly related to the strength of the updraft and that, in turn, depends on the size and vigor of the convective cell. An ordinary cumulonimbus cloud usually releases hailstones about the size of peppercorns. In a supercell, where many times more energy is being used, hailstones can sometimes grow very much bigger. There have been many reports of hailstones the size of golf balls and bigger. Fortunately, these rarely cause much damage because there are few of them. Most hailstones are caught in the downcurrent before they can grow to this size. What does cause damage is the intensity of a supercell hailstorm in which individual hailstones are quite small, but fall in huge numbers and are accelerated toward the ground by the downdraft carrying them. They can strip the ears from corn and cereal crops. A scientist once traced the path of a particular storm from fields identified by the farmers who filed insurance claims for damage to the crops in them.

The diagram gives the misleading impression that the upcurrents and downcurrents flow like winds. You might imagine the air blowing directly along invisible tunnels, with the flow in a direction parallel to the tunnels themselves. In fact, the air spirals its way upward and downward through the storm, usually moving counterclockwise.

This rotation starts where wind shear deflects the upcurrent, usually at about the mid-height of the cloud. Moving air (and liquid) has a natural tendency to turn around an axis at right angles to its direction of movement. This behavior is called *vorticity* (see below) and it spreads downward from the middle of the cloud, where the upcurrent is bending away from the vertical, until it sets the whole of the mesocyclone beneath it rotating all the way to the bottom of the cloud.

Rotation at the base of the mesocyclone is what makes fragments of cloud turn, and as it speeds up, part of the cloud descends below the base of the main cloud. This descended cloud, projecting from the rear of the storm, turning slowly, and from which no rain falls, is what appears as a wall cloud. To people far enough away to see the whole width of the storm passing across their line of sight it is clearly marked as a solid-looking cloud attached to the bottom of the main cloud. It is not a tornado, but it is beneath the wall cloud that tornadoes may appear.

Vortices and angular momentum

Have you ever wondered how a soldier manages to steer a tank? You steer a car by changing the direction in which its front wheels point, but tanks run on caterpillar tracks and they have neither front wheels nor steering wheels. All the same, tanks can turn corners. This is possible because tank tracks can be controlled independently to run at different speeds. The tank turns when the driver slows down or speeds up the track on one side. This makes the tank follow a path that curves in the direction of the slower track. You steer a rowboat in the same way. Row on one side of the boat only and the boat will turn away from the side you are rowing. Taxiing airliners also steer by means of their engines. In each of these cases, increasing or decreasing power to one side makes the two sides of the tank, boat, or plane try to move at different speeds and the result is a turn in the direction of the slower side.

There is a general rule here rather similar to one that applies to liquids and gases. If there are two streams, side by side and flowing in the same direction but a different speeds, the faster stream will curve in the direction of the slower. When air (or water) moves it does so in relation to the air (or water) to either side. This means there is always a stream flowing faster than the stream next to it (which may not be moving at all) and, therefore, all moving streams will tend to follow curved paths. Assuming there is nothing confining them, such as the banks of a river or the sides of a valley, streams will eventually flow more or less in circles. This tendency of a moving stream to curve is called *vorticity*. Vorticity may cause the moving gas or liquid to rotate about any axis, but since winds, rivers, and ocean currents flow horizontally the most important axes are vertical. The flow that affects weather systems, including tornadoes, tends to make air rotate about a vertical axis.

The Earth, too, is moving as it spins on its axis and this motion also deflects moving liquids and gases into curved paths, due to the Coriolis effect (see box on page 50). Coriolis deflection induces vorticity and, because its vorticity is due to the movement of the planet, it is called *planetary vorticity*.

Planetary vorticity is significant only where the movement is large. It affects air masses moving across continents and oceans, but very small streams, flowing only a short distance, also curve. They have a vorticity of their own.

There is an example of this that is familiar to everyone. When water flows out of a bathtub it usually forms a spiral as it goes down the drain and the closer it is to the hole the faster it turns. The bathwater spirals because of its own vorticity and it is easy to understand why. It is flowing downhill toward a small hole and you can picture it as forming many small streams flowing side by side. Those near the center of the tub are rushing to fill the drain, and those near the sides are slowed by friction against the sides of the tub. They form parallel streams flowing at different speeds, and so the faster streams tend to curve in the direction of the slower ones until they form a circle or, in this case, a spiral called a *vortex*. This is very like the way a tornado spins.

Many people believe that water spirals down the drain counter-clockwise in the northern hemisphere and clockwise in the

The Coriolis effect

Any object moving toward or away from the equator and not firmly attached to the surface does not travel in a straight line. It is deflected to the right in the northern hemisphere and to the left in the southern hemisphere. Moving air and water tend to follow a clockwise path in the northern hemisphere and a counterclockwise path in the southern hemisphere.

The reason for this was discovered in 1835 by the French physicist Gaspard Gustave de Coriolis and it is called the *Coriolis effect*. It happens because the Earth is a rotating sphere and as an object moves above the surface, the Earth below is also moving. The effect used to be called the Coriolis *force*, but it is not a force. It results simply from the fact that we observe motion in relation to fixed points on the surface. The effect is easily demonstrated by the simple experiment described in volume 6.

The Earth makes one complete turn on its axis every 24 hours. This means every point on the surface is constantly moving and returns to its original position (relative to the Sun) every 24 hours, but different points on the surface travel different distances to do so. Consider two points on the surface, one at the equator and the other at 40° N, which is the

The Coriolis effect.

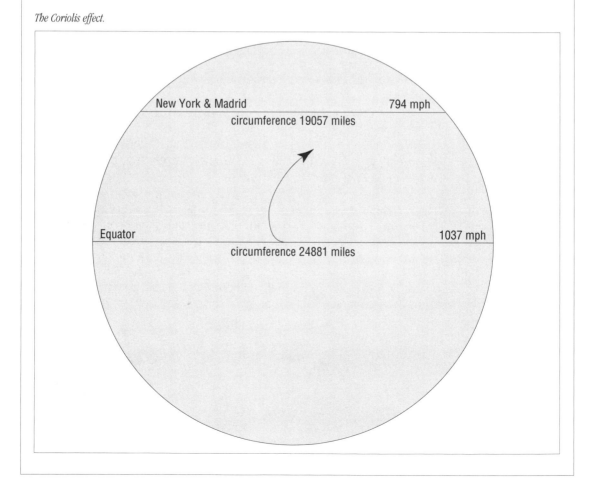

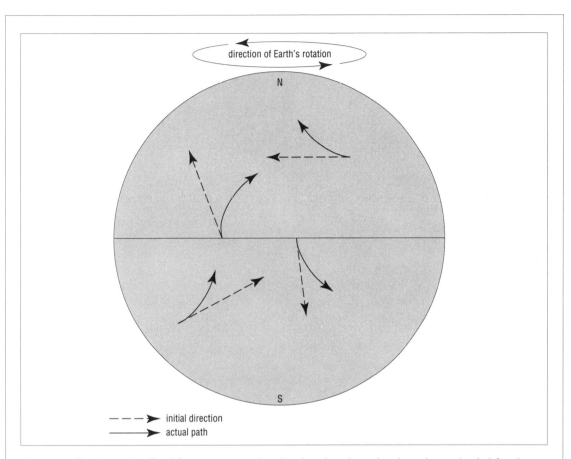

The Coriolis effect: The Coriolis effect deflects air masses and winds to the right in the northern hemisphere and to the left in the southern hemisphere. It has no effect at the equator and maximum effect at the poles.

approximate latitude of New York and Madrid. The equator, latitude 0°, is about 24,881 miles long. That is how far a point on the equator must travel in 24 hours, which means it moves at about 1,037 MPH. At 40° N, the circumference parallel to the equator is about 19,057 miles. The point there has less distance to travel and so it moves at about 794 MPH.

Suppose you planned to fly an aircraft to New York from the point on the equator due south of New York (and could ignore the winds). If you headed due north you would not reach New York. At the Equator you are already traveling eastward at 1,037 MPH. As you fly north, the surface beneath you is also traveling east, but at a slower speed the farther you travel. If the journey from 0° to 40° N took you 6 hours, in that time you would also move about 6,000 miles to the east relative to the position of the surface beneath you, but the surface itself would also move, at New York by about 4,700 miles, so you would end not at New York, but (6,000 - 4,700 =) 1,300 miles to the east of New York, way out over the Atlantic.

The size of the Coriolis effect is directly proportional to the speed at which the body moves and its latitude. The effect on a body moving at 100 MPH is ten times greater than that on one moving at 10 MPH, and the Coriolis effect is greatest at the poles and zero at the equator.

southern. Some go even further, and would have you believe you can tell which hemisphere you are in by the way the water leaves the bathtub, because the direction changes the instant you cross the equator. It is a lovely idea, but very unreliable. You can test it for yourself. Each time you take a bath, make a note of the way the water spirals. Over a large number of trials you will find you have recorded about as many clockwise spirals as counterclockwise ones.

Water spirals down the drain because of its own vorticity, not planetary vorticity. If the tub were the size of an ocean, then the Coriolis effect would determine the direction in which the water turned, but a real bathtub is far too small to be influenced in this way. Even if it were, there is no Coriolis effect at the equator, so tropical bathtubs would be no help in telling you where you were, although water spirals out of them there as it does everywhere.

Vorticity therefore has two components. There is planetary vorticity and the vorticity of the moving stream itself. This is known as *relative vorticity*. Add the two together and the result is called the *absolute vorticity*. Absolute vorticity tells you how a moving stream will really behave. Planetary vorticity deflects streams to the right in the northern hemisphere and to the left in the southern. This is called *cyclonic* motion and, by convention, it is known as *positive vorticity*. Cyclonic flow moves counterclockwise in the northern hemisphere and clockwise in the southern. Rotation in the opposite directions is called *anticyclonic* and results from *negative vorticity*.

On a scale large enough for planetary vorticity to be significant, if relative vorticity is positive it adds to planetary vorticity so the absolute vorticity will be the sum of the two. If relative vorticity is negative, on the other hand, it may disappear altogether, over-whelmed by the much stronger planetary vorticity acting in the opposite direction and from which it must be subtracted.

Air converges into an area of low pressure, for which the technical term is a *cyclone*, and its convergence produces a cyclonic flow that increases in strength as long as the convergence continues. This produces a strongly positive absolute vorticity. Diverging air, flowing away from an area of high pressure, or *anticyclone*, has negative relative vorticity and provided the divergence continues at a constant rate, its absolute vorticity decreases, eventually to zero. (Bath water converges as it approaches the drain. In the northern hemisphere this tends to swing it counterclockwise, but the amount of water is so small that the effects is negligible and it is liable to rotate in either direction.)

Inside a supercell, or each of the convective cells in a multicell cloud, air is moving rapidly upward in the upcurrents. This draws in air at the base. Air flowing inward is converging over a distance large enough for planetary vorticity to be significant, so as the air is drawn into the cloud it acquires positive absolute vorticity. In other words, it starts to spin in a counterclockwise direction (in the northern hemisphere) around its own axis and it continues spinning as it rises, moving in an upward spiral. Wind shear aloft sets the rising column rotating in the middle of the cloud, but the positive vorticity of the converging air increases the rate of spin. In the northern hemisphere almost all tornadoes spin counterclockwise, although occasionally they have been known to spin clockwise. Scientists believe clockwise tornadoes are set spinning by the downcurrent from the supercell.

At the top of the cloud, rising air forms a region of high pressure. Air flows away from it. This is divergence, with negative relative vorticity, and so its absolute vorticity is very small. The outflowing air flows in more or less straight lines, rapidly carrying air away from the top of the upcurrents and drawing more air upward to take its place.

Now another effect becomes influential. This has the forbidding name of the *conservation of angular momentum*. The principle is much less alarming than it sounds.

Three factors are involved when any body spins about its own axis. These are the mass of the body (on Earth this is equivalent to its weight), its spinning radius, and the rate at which it is turning. This is measured as the number of degrees through which it turns in a given time and is known as its *angular velocity*. The Earth, for example, makes one complete turn, through 360°, every 24 hours, so it has an angular velocity of $360 \div 24 = 15°$ per hour. If you multiply these three factors together, mass × radius × angular velocity, the product is a number that remains constant should any of the factors change. If one of the factors increases, for example, one or both of the others must decrease so the product remains the same when they are multiplied together. Suppose an orbiting satellite that is spinning around the center of the Earth broke in two. Each piece would have less mass than the whole satellite. To conserve angular momentum the pieces might accelerate to increase their angular velocity, or move into higher orbits to increase their orbital radius.

There is a more familiar example that you may have seen. Figure skaters often perform accelerating pirouettes. The skater starts the spin with her arms fully outstretched. Once the spin has begun, she gradually draws in her arms toward her body. As she does so she spins faster. Her spin accelerates because by withdrawing her arms she reduces her radius of spin. To conserve her angular momentum either her mass or her angular velocity must increase. Clearly, she cannot suddenly gain weight, so she spins faster. The spin accelerates without any extra effort from her. It is an entirely automatic consequence of reducing her spin radius. If this strikes you as improbable, you need not attempt figure skating to demonstrate the effect for yourself. Experiment 5 in volume 6 explains how to do so quite simply.

Think now of the shape of a tornado. It extends from the base of the cloud to the ground and is much narrower at the bottom than at the top. This is only the visible part of the tornado. It also extends upward to about the middle of the cloud, and it is spinning all the way. It is a vortex like a drain, but upside down because it draws air upward. Low pressure stretches the vortex downward (see page 56 for an explanation of why this happens). Stretching makes the funnel taper, but it does not alter the mass of air at each level within it. Tapering reduces the radius of the vortex.

The vortex is a mass of air that starts rotating in the middle of the cloud. It forms in an upcurrent, through which air is rising, but the rotating mass remains. The upcurrent merely feeds it by adding air at the bottom as it is removed at the top. What matters is the rotation, not the fact that individual air molecules are moving through the vortex.

When the air in the middle of the cloud starts to rotate it has a certain mass, a certain angular velocity (rate of spin), and a certain radius. If any one of these is altered the others must change as well in order to conserve angular momentum. The tornado forms when the vortex is drawn toward the ground and tapers as a result of stretching. Figure 20 illustrates the way its angular momentum is conserved. The mass of the air remains unchanged, but tapering reduces its radius, and therefore its angular velocity increases at the narrow bottom of the funnel. In the center of the cloud, at the top of the vortex, the air is turning relatively slowly, but at ground level it is turning at a ferocious speed and the air being drawn into it is accelerated by its own convergence to the same rotational speed.

The tremendous winds of a tornado result from vorticity and the conservation of angular momentum. The effect is the same as that which makes a figure skater spin faster when she draws in her arms.

Structure of a tornado

When you think about it, it seems odd that a liquid can be made to move uphill. Yet this is what happens when you suck a drink through a straw. The drink moves up the straw. Inside the glass or can, the weight of the atmosphere exerts the same amount of pressure on every part of the surface of the drink. Sucking reduces the air pressure inside the straw and, therefore, the pressure acting on the drink at the bottom of the straw. It is being pushed down less strongly there than everywhere else, so it rises. To put this another way, the liquid moves from a region of relatively high pressure to one of relatively low pressure, in this case your mouth.

Figure 19: *A tornado.* (National Center for Atmospheric Research, Boulder, CO)

A supercell is rather like a drinking straw, with the divergence of air at the top doing the sucking. Air is sucked upward. It spins as it rises because there is so much of it. If you could suck on a straw about six miles across, your drink would spin through the straw, too. Air rushes into the bottom of the supercell and if the individual molecules of your drink were big enough to be visible, you would see them rushing toward the bottom of the straw in just the same way, sweeping tiny dust particles along with them and up into straw, like a tornado picking up debris.

The harder you suck on a straw the faster the drink flows into your mouth, because the harder you suck the lower you make the air pressure in the straw. How fast the drink flows depends on the difference between the air pressure at the bottom of the straw and the air pressure surrounding it.

Tornadoes are also driven by differences in air pressure, but with a difference. When you drink from a straw the vertical distance between your head and the bottom of the straw is very small, but the top of a tornado vortex is a considerable distance above ground level. This is important because of the decrease of atmospheric pressure with height.

Pressure is lowest at the center of the vortex. As the bottom of the vortex reaches the base of the wall cloud the pressure at its center may be about 100 millibars lower than the ground-level atmospheric pressure well clear of the vortex. This amounts to a difference of only 1.5 pounds per square inch. It sounds very small, but it makes the core pressure equal to the ordinary atmospheric pressure at a height of about 3,000 feet. That is enough to pull part of the wall cloud all the way to the ground. The tornado is an extension of the wall cloud.

As it descends, the tornado funnel consists only of air, but it is moist air and the pressure within it is very low, making the water vapor it carries condense into liquid droplets. These are exactly similar to cloud droplets, but they form in the tornado funnel and are not part of the cloud itself. How much water vapor condenses depends on the amount the air contains and this varies. It is the water droplets that make the descending funnel visible, and therefore most funnels are white, the color of cloud droplets. Storm clouds look black only because they contain so many droplets they block out a considerable proportion of the sunlight, making the sky dark, but the droplets themselves are not black.

Not all tornadoes appear as clearly defined white funnels, however. If the air descending in the funnel is relatively dry there will be less condensation in it than in moister air. The density of water droplets in the funnel will be low, and the funnel will appear faint. It may even be invisible. Other tornadoes form behind heavy rain, which hides them.

Even then, they often reveal themselves. Before the funnel reaches the ground, the air at ground level is already rotating vigorously as it is drawn into the upcurrent. Its rotation raises a cloud of dust and small debris to a height of a few tens of feet and a few hundred yards wide. This cloud is often visible from a considerable distance, provided, of course, the visibility is not reduced by rain. If you see a cloud of this kind in the distance, apparently sitting on the ground with a dark storm cloud low above it, expect a tornado at any moment, because the funnel has already started its descent. Many tornadoes fail to develop, so it may not complete its descent all the way to the ground before disappearing, but even if that one fails another may be about to appear nearby.

Whether you can see it or not, you are very likely to hear it. When so much air moves with so much energy it makes a great deal of noise. At a distance, the rumbling, roaring sound is like that of a freight train.

Soon after it touches the ground, the color of the funnel changes. Air flowing into the base of the upcurrent with the force of a gale carries dust, dirt, and any loose material in its path, sending it all spiraling upward and making the funnel brown or gray, and light or dark depending on the material coloring it, and eventually enveloping the funnel in a cloud of dust. Fully developed, the tornado may retain its funnel shape, but the dust cloud surrounding it may alter its appearance greatly. A tornado can look like a ballooning cloud. While it is forming its funnel descends more or less vertically, but in most cases its alignment quickly changes. The funnel curves over, often until its upper part is almost horizontal, and it twists and snakes as it moves.

At its center, the vortex is open and the air clear, like the eye of a hurricane. Around the eye, wind speeds can exceed 200 MPH and

Figure 20: *Tornadoes and the conservation of angular momentum. As the rotating air at the center of the cloud stretches downward, it becomes narrower. This reduces its radius of rotation and so its angular velocity increases.*

sometimes reach more than 300 MPH, though it is understandably difficult to make precise measurements. At its base, the funnel is up to about 400 yards across, but can be much smaller. Most of the damage a tornado causes is due to the force of its winds, but it is the difference in pressure and the fierce upcurrent that lifts large objects, sometimes to a considerable height. The tornado itself is moving forward (see page 61) and so the objects it lifts are carried with it. This is how they can be transported from one place to another.

Tornadoes are renowned for their freakish effects. Some of these are due not to the main tornado, but to smaller ones that surround it and are triggered by it. These are called *suction vortices* and are often hidden in the dust cloud surrounding the base of the main tornado.

Air rushing in to join the upcurrent crosses uneven ground and encounters buildings, trees, and other obstacles. Some of these it destroys, but it expends some of its energy doing so and is deflected from its course. The airflow is by no means as even as you might expect it to be. The wind gusts change direction this way and that, and make all the moving air extremely turbulent. Turbulence produces eddies, like the eddies you can make by drawing your hand through water, but these eddies form in air that is already rotating strongly and accelerating as it approaches the vortex.

Eddies can rotate in either direction, but some of them turn cyclonically, in the same counterclockwise direction as the wall cloud and the tornado reaching down from it. They have their own rotational speed, or angular velocity, but they also have the angular velocity of the main tornado and the mesocyclone above it, as well as the forward movement of the tornado. All of these add to their speed, which means they turn much faster than the tornado itself. If the tornado generates winds of 200 MPH, its suction vortices can blow at 300 MPH.

They are very small, some no more than 10 feet across, and few ever reach a diameter of more than 100 feet. They are also short-lived. Few last longer than about three minutes. They travel around their parent tornado, in the same direction as it is spinning, usually counterclockwise, but rarely complete even one full orbit. Finally, because they form so close to their parent tornado, they are often hidden inside its dust cloud. No one sees them as they come and go. No one hears them, either, in the general screaming, roaring tumult of the storm.

In most cases it is only after they pass that evidence can be found for their brief existence, although they have been seen and even photographed. On April 10, 1979, a tornado at Wichita Falls, Texas, produced six suction vortices, and they show clearly in a photograph. That tornado, or set of tornadoes, destroyed nearly 8,000 homes and killed 44 people.

Sometimes a suction vortex strikes a house, but it is so small that only part of the house is damaged by it. Suction vortices have been known to demolish half a house, leaving the remainder untouched, and then vanish before reaching the neighboring house, so the damaged house stands by itself amid undamaged houses. When they move over crops they make spiral or circular patterns. They may be responsible for some of the "crop circles" that from time to time make the news in Europe (but most are deliberate hoaxes) and they have also left long, spiraling tracks of flattened corn. Where they occur on open ground they can make shallow holes, just a few feet across, by drawing up dirt from the surface. At one time, people believed these suction scars were the footprints of giants.

Figure 21: *Tornado damage.* (National Center for Atmospheric Research, Boulder, CO)

What happens inside a tornado

Few people have gazed into the heart of a tornado and lived to tell what they saw. Yet there are a very few exceptions. In 1991, a man was sitting in his car in Colorado when a tornado passed directly over him. True, he did not look upward into it, but he did experience the passing of the funnel. It began, he reported, in absolute calm. Then the car was hit by what he described as a "slam of wind" and hailstones the size of marbles and he ducked, fearing the windows of the car would be smashed. The wind, which he guessed was moving faster than 70 MPH, ceased almost at once. He looked out and there was the funnel.

One person who did stare directly into a tornado funnel was able to do so safely because, as it approached, the funnel lifted from the ground. Tornadoes are dangerous only while they are touching the ground. Once the bottom of the funnel lifts, it loses contact with the buildings and other structures and objects it can destroy. It still twists and roars, but it is harmless.

This does not mean you can afford to take risks. If you see an approaching tornado lift above the ground, on no account wait for a chance to gaze into it. Tornadoes often raise themselves in this way, only to descend to ground level again in a matter of moments. The apparently safe tornado coming toward you could have turned back into a killer by the time it reaches you. Will Keller knew what he was doing.

Keller was a Kansas farmer, working in his fields one June afternoon in 1928 when he saw a tornado moving toward him. He called his family together and led them to the prepared cellar. They entered and he was about to follow them and shut the door when he glanced back at the tornado. It was now quite close, but he saw that its base was lifting clear of the ground. He knew this meant the tornado would not harm him, but also that he could jump into the cellar in an instant if the base started to descend again.

The tornado continued to lift as slowly it approached until it was directly overhead and Mr. Keller found himself gazing straight up into its funnel. He said the air was very still, but the end of the funnel made a loud hissing noise. There was a strong smell that he described as "gassy" and he found it difficult to breathe. The smell may well have been of ozone. Ozone is a form of oxygen (O_3), with a strong, acrid smell; it causes breathing difficulty in very small doses. Electric sparks can produce it by supplying the energy to break apart oxygen molecules ($O_2 \rightarrow O + O$), some oxygen atoms then combining with oxygen molecules to form ozone ($O + O_2 \rightarrow O_3$).

Tornadoes appear beneath storm clouds in which there is a great deal of electrical activity and lightning sparks big enough to produce plenty of ozone. It was the lightning, constantly flashing across the inside of the funnel, that allowed Mr. Keller to see what was happening. He reckoned the base was 50 to 100 feet across, and he was able to see up it to a height of at least 2,500 feet. Its walls were clouds rotating about the center. The hissing noise was made by small tornadoes that were forming like tails around the lower rim of the funnel, breaking away, and disappearing. The funnel itself, he said, was rotating counterclockwise, but some of the "tails" rotated counterclockwise, others clockwise.

Like the eye of a hurricane, the center of a tornado funnel is fairly calm, with air descending slowly through it, and the atmospheric pressure is very low. This core is surrounded by air spiraling upward, and it is here that the winds occur. Clouds form as moist air is drawn into the spiral, the pressure falls abruptly, and its water vapor condenses. Wind speeds fall with increasing distance from the core.

Electrical activity is intense. The base of the parent supercell carries a negative charge and sparking between this and the positive charge at a higher level probably accounts for much of the lightning seen inside the tornado funnel, but it is also possible that the rapid rotation of the funnel acts like a dynamo, generating its own electricity.

Sometimes the entire funnel is illuminated. People watching from several miles away said a tornado in Oklahoma in May 1955 had what looked like a pinwheel of fire spinning at its top. Others said the funnel was lit from inside, blue near the top and orange lower down, with orange fire spitting from its base.

So far, scientists do not have a complete explanation for these lights, but there have been reports of them since Old Testament times. The prophet Ezekiel certainly knew about them. "And I looked, and, behold, a whirlwind came out of the north, a great cloud, and a fire infolding itself, and a brightness was about it, and out of the midst thereof as the color of amber, out of the midst of the fire." (Ezekiel 1:4.)

How a tornado travels

Watch the ordinary cumulus clouds that often dot the sky on a fine afternoon like tangles of clean cotton wool as they drift across the sky, carried by the wind. Check their direction with a nearby wind vane and usually you find the clouds are traveling in a different direction from the way the vane points. It is the wind at the height of the clouds that carries them, not the wind at ground level.

Cumulonimbus storm clouds are very much bigger. It is more difficult to see them move because they occupy such a large proportion of the sky. All the same, they do move and, like the smaller cumulus, it is the wind that carries them. In their case, it is the wind at about the height of the middle of the cloud. With a massive storm cloud this will be the wind at around 20,000 feet.

Clouds that produce tornadoes move rather differently. Like an ordinary thunderstorm, a multicell storm cloud is driven by the wind at about 20,000 feet. The cloud as a whole moves with the mid-altitude wind and air flows into it from its right, at an angle of about 45°. Multicell clouds are deceptive, however. In them, the upcurrents are repeatedly stifled by their own downcurrents and sinking air spills to the right of the direction in which the cloud itself is moving. This spillage triggers a new upcurrent, which becomes a new convection cell to the right of the previous one. The old cell then dies. As figure 22A shows, the result is a series of steps in which, relative to the direction of its forward motion, the active convection cell shifts diagonally to the right.

Although cells are dying all the time and are being replaced by new ones forming next to them, the individual cells are not obviously visible, and that is what makes these clouds deceptive. What you see is just one huge storm cloud. Overall, therefore, the apparent effect is that the storm travels to the right of the mid-altitude wind. In other words, a multicell cumulonimbus seems to move almost directly into the inflowing wind. Provided meteorologists can track the movement of the whole storm cloud and measure the direction of the inflowing air, this allows them to distinguish an ordinary, single-cell thunderstorm from a multicell cumulonimbus and to calculate from the inflow the direction in which the storm cloud is moving.

Multicell storms often develop along squall lines (see page 24). This adds a further complication because the cold front producing the squall line is also moving. Most weather fronts travel in a generally easterly direction in the middle latitudes of both hemispheres. They are propelled by the high-level winds, which in these

Figure 22:
a) *Direction of movement of a multicell storm.*
b) *Direction of movement of a supercell storm.*

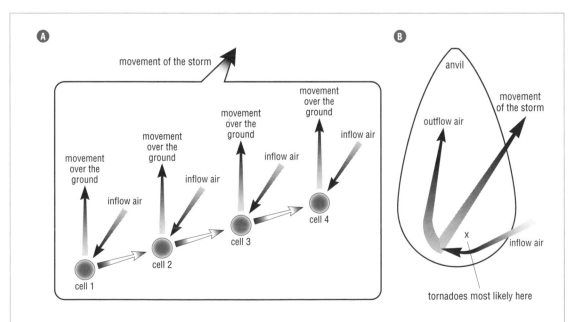

latitudes are westerlies (blowing from west to east). Over the United States, they are from the southwest. Since this is the direction the cold front travels, it is also the direction of travel of its associated squall line and the storms along it. In 1925, for example, a very severe outbreak of about seven tornadoes started in Missouri, then moved northeastward across Illinois and Indiana for a total distance of nearly 440 miles. The squall line that produced the 1974 Super Outbreak traveled eastward and was very long. At one point it extended from the Gulf of Mexico into Canada and 148 tornadoes occurred at various points along it. Individual storms move with the front that causes them, but at the same time they move with the mid-altitude wind and apparently shift to the right of it because of the continual formation of new cells. The result is that the squall line as a whole moves in a generally easterly direction, but the storms it produces tend to move along the front. This means tornadoes can occur anywhere along a cold front that has a squall line.

Although in North America the high-level westerlies usually blow from southwest to northeast, occasionally in late spring and early summer they blow from the northwest and the storms move the other way. On May 27, 1896, for example, an outbreak of 18 tornadoes around St. Louis, Missouri, traveled from northwest to southeast.

A supercell cumulonimbus is very like an ordinary cumulonimbus in many respects, so you might expect it to travel the same way, in the direction of the mid-altitude wind. Some supercells do, but most do not. For reasons scientists are so far unable to explain, most supercell storms travel in a direction to the right of the mid-altitude wind and a few travel to the left of it. If you can see the direction the anvil points, this indicates the direction in which air is being swept away from the upcurrents. This is approximately at right angles to the direction of inflowing air. A supercell cloud usually travels at about 45° to the right (shown in figure 22B), or more rarely left, of the axis of the anvil.

Not all supercell storms need fronts to trigger their development. Isolated ones can form wherever the ground is heated strongly by the Sun and the air is moist. There is no front to direct their movement, but nevertheless the mid-altitude wind that drives them forward is often westerly, so they, like multicell storms, tend to move from west to east.

Supercell storms usually last for several hours. This is much longer than the lifespan of an ordinary storm cloud, but still it is not very long. They move fast, however, and during their brief lives they can travel tens of miles, their hail, rain, and tornadoes wreaking havoc as they go.

Squall lines live for much longer and a single squall line can carry 50 or more multicell cumulonimbus clouds spread along it. During the period in which it was generating tornadoes, the 1974 Super Outbreak squall line traveled more than 550 miles in 16 hours and 10 minutes, at an average speed of about 35 MPH.

The movement of isolated supercell clouds and squall-line cold fronts can be tracked and people can be given ample warning of their approach, but predicting the track of an individual tornado is much more difficult. They form beneath storm clouds, but their movement over the ground is very erratic. Most of those associated with a cold front move along the front, parallel to it, traveling from southwest to northeast, which is the usual orientation of cold fronts, but this is no more than a generalization, and there are many exceptions. Some tornadoes stay over one spot, hardly moving at all. Others move in circles, or describe figure eights, and they can change the pattern without warning. If you see a tornado, even in what seems to be the far distance and stationary, the only sensible rule is to assume it will come for you and take appropriate action. With tornadoes, safety lies in expecting the worst while hoping for the best.

Their tracks are erratic and their speeds and the distances they cover no less so. Obviously, those which are stationary have no forward speed. Most move at between about 25 and 40 MPH. In 1977, a tornado crossed Illinois and Indiana at an average speed of 46 MPH, covering 340 miles in 7 hours and 20 minutes. It is not unknown, however, for a tornado to travel at 65 MPH.

Tornadoes seldom last very long, so even if they travel fast they rarely have time to travel very far. Few cover more than 25 miles. The average track of the tornadoes in the 1974 Super Outbreak was 18.7 miles, which was thought to be rather long. In 1973, the average track length for all tornadoes in the United States was 4.7 miles and in 1972 it was 3.3 miles. Even so, there are exceptions. The 340-mile track of the 1977 tornado may be the longest ever recorded, but the Tri-State Outbreak (so called because it crossed the three states of Missouri, Illinois, and Indiana) in March 1925 included one tornado that traveled 219 miles at 60 MPH. In April 1908 an outbreak in Louisiana and Georgia included one tornado that covered 158 miles, from Weiss, Louisiana, to Winchester, Mississippi, at about 45 MPH.

The distance a tornado travels depends, at least partly, on the terrain it covers. They move best over level, open ground and tend to dissipate when they meet hills and steep-sided valleys. There are exceptions, as you might expect, for tornadoes with more energy than most. One of the Super Outbreak tornadoes was seen to descend to the bottom of a canyon, 1,000 feet deep, cross it, and climb 3,300 feet to the top of the ridge on the other side. It was estimated that the winds around the core of that tornado may have reached about 260 MPH. It was so energetic even a large canyon could not stop it.

At its base, a tornado funnel is narrow. It is the diameter of the funnel base that determines the width of the track a tornado makes. Damage occurs only within this track and tornadoes are almost surgically precise. Properties even a foot or two outside the track are likely to be unharmed by the wind, although they may be severely damaged by debris dropped from a considerable height or hurled with great force. Few tracks are more than about half a mile wide and the width of many is no more than 100 to 400 yards. There is always a tornado that breaks the rules, of course. For part of its journey, the track of the 1908 Louisiana-Georgia tornado, which covered 158 miles, was 2.5 miles wide.

Although most tracks are narrow, tornadoes often occur in groups with overlapping tracks, so the actual trail of damage is much wider. Suction vortices (see page 58) just outside the main funnel can cause appalling damage, but full-scale tornadoes can divide into several separate funnels and adjacent funnels can merge. This produces confused tracks that vary greatly in width from place to place. A tornado that struck Viroqua, Wisconsin, in 1865 comprised several main vortices that later merged into a single funnel, and in April 1974, Tanner, Alabama, was hit by two tornadoes that arrived half an hour apart.

How a tornado dies

Tornadoes rarely live for very long. The one in 1977 that lasted more than seven hours and traveled some 340 miles across Illinois and Indiana was very unusual. Few last longer than 20 minutes and many disappear within one minute or less. One consequence of this is that many tornadoes go unreported. They occur in remote, sparsely populated areas, disappear quickly, and no one notices them until later, when the damage they caused to plants is discovered and the culprit identified.

How long a tornado lasts depends on the energy available to it. The more energy it has, the more intense it will be. This suggests that severe tornadoes are likely to continue for longer than mild ones, but many intense tornadoes divide into several vortices, sharing the total amount of energy among them. Once this happens, the individually weaker tornadoes may dissipate quickly, but two or more of them may rejoin, combining their energy once more. As always with tornadoes, it is impossible to predict their behavior at all accurately.

They represent a huge concentration of energy. It is not that they release so much. An ordinary summer shower releases ten times more energy than an average tornado and most thunderstorms release 1,000 times more without being thought especially severe. The ferocity of a tornado is due entirely to its ability to concentrate energy into a small area. The volume of an average thunderstorm cumulonimbus is about 280 cubic miles and that of an average tornado about one cubic mile. Suppose the thunderstorm has an energy of 1,000 (the units do not matter) and the tornado of 1, to allow for the fact that the thunderstorm has 1,000 times more energy than the tornado. The energy of the thunderstorm, distributed throughout its 280 cubic miles, has a concentration (or "energy density") of about 0.3 per cubic mile. The tornado has an energy of one per cubic mile. Its energy density is more than three times greater than that of the thunderstorm and the energy density of a thunderstorm is already high.

What is remarkable is not that the life of a tornado is so brief, but that enough energy can be concentrated for it to form in the first place. Huge concentrations of energy are difficult to achieve and almost always unstable. Think what happens when you boil water to make coffee, for example. Heating the water increases its energy. The boiling water has more energy than the surrounding air, because the air is much cooler than the water, so the hot water represents a concentration of energy, or, to put it another way, it has a higher energy density. The increase was achieved by burning fuel to "pump" energy into it. Once you have made the coffee, however, it starts to cool at once. Unless you drink it while it is hot it will continue to cool until it is at the same temperature as the air in the room (which will have been warmed by it, but so slightly you will not notice the effect). The concentration of energy was difficult to achieve and unstable.

This instability occurs because energy always flows from regions of higher concentration to regions of lower concentration. Heating cold water until it boils does not contradict this principle, because the stove on which the water is heated also has a high energy density and energy flows from it to the lower energy density of the water. The stove, in its turn, is heated by burning fuel, which has an even higher energy density. That energy flows in only one direction is one of the most basic of scientific principles, known as the second law of thermodynamics (see box on page 67).

A tornado requires a large additional concentration of energy, which occurs when the drop in pressure between outside air and air in the center of the vortex of rising air (the pressure gradient) is more than 8 millibars per 100 feet. Such a sharp drop to so low a core pressure is very rarely attained. Some scientists believe electrical discharges inside the funnel may provide some of the energy driving the movement of air that produces the low pressure, but they do not know how this might work.

It cannot last. Air spills into the low-pressure core, raising its pressure. This starts at the bottom of the funnel, where it is narrowest

The laws of thermodynamics

Thermodynamics is the scientific study of energy, the ways it can be transformed from one form into another, the ways it moves, and its ability to do work. All of these are governed by four laws of thermodynamics. Their numbering is unusual. Laws 1 and 2 were discovered in 1850 by the German physicist Rudolf Clausius (1822–88). He developed the first law from earlier work by the French physicist Nicolas Léonard Sadi Carnot (1796–1832) and the English physicist James Prescott Joule (1818–89). This led him and William Thomson (Lord Kelvin, 1824–1907) to the second law. The third law was discovered in 1906 by the German physical chemist Walter Hermann Nernst (1864–1941), for which he was awarded the 1920 Nobel Prize in Chemistry. Another principle, which follows from the second law and had been accepted for centuries, was recognized later as a law of thermodynamics. It was more fundamental than the others, however, so could not properly be called the fourth law. At the same time, renumbering the three established laws would cause confusion. The English physicist Sir Ralph Howard Fowler (1889–1944) proposed it be called the zeroth law.

0 (the zeroth law) This states that if two bodies are in thermal equilibrium (e.g., at the same temperature) as each other and both are in thermal equilibrium with a third body, then all three are in thermal equilibrium and no energy will pass among them. This is the most fundamental of the laws.

1 (the first law) This states that energy can be neither created or lost, but it can change its form (e.g., chemical energy in a fuel can be changed to heat, and in an engine heat can be changed into motion). The first law is often called the Law of the Conservation of Energy, because this follows from it. The law also proves the impossibility of a perpetual motion machine, because energy cannot be created to power it.

2 (the second law) This states that heat cannot move from one body to another body at a higher temperature without producing some other effect. For example, if two bodies at different temperatures are placed side by side, the temperature of the cooler will rise and that of the warmer fall until both are at the same temperature (if you leave a cup of coffee standing on the table, it will cool until it is at room temperature; it never grows hotter and the air in the room never grows cooler). Heat pumps, refrigerators, and freezers remove heat from a cool body and pass it to a warmer body, but this does not contradict the second law, because work is done to effect the transfer of heat. The second law also means that where energy is concentrated it will flow to regions of lower concentration until it becomes evenly distributed. This dispersion of energy is called *entropy*.

3 (the third law) This states that in a perfectly crystalline solid there is a temperature at which no further change in entropy occurs. This temperature is called "absolute zero," 0 on the kelvin (K) scale (1K = 1° C = 1.8° F; 0K = -273.15° C = -459.67° F). Absolute zero cannot be attained, although modern physicists have cooled substances to within a few millionths of a degree of it.

and the pressure gradient steepest. Many tornadoes start to weaken when they cross uneven ground, perhaps because friction with the rough surface slows the inflowing air and causes eddies that spill air directly into the base of the vortex. Towns usually destroy tornadoes in this way, although not before suffering damage. There are exceptions, of course. On June 13, 1968, a tornado appeared 8 miles southwest of Tracy, Minnesota, and traveled northeast at 35 MPH for a distance of 13 miles. It passed right through the town, without lifting from the ground, killing nine people, injuring 125, and leaving a trail of damage 300 to 500 feet wide that cost $3 million.

As it fills with air, the bottom of the funnel disappears. It looks as though the funnel raises itself above the ground, but in fact the lower part of the funnel has filled with air and vanished. Air is still swirling into the funnel, but it is air drawn from above ground level and it has no effect on objects on the ground. As Will Keller knew when he gazed up into a funnel in 1928 (see page 60), once its funnel no longer reaches all the way to the ground, a tornado is harmless and below it the air is relatively calm.

Unless the funnel descends again, which some do, the tornado is now doomed. Its energy dissipates as air pressure in the core equalizes with that outside. When the core pressure is no longer low enough to make water vapor condense in the inflowing air, the funnel fades. Soon after that, the concentration of energy driving the tornado is lost, the energy of the storm becomes more evenly distributed, and the tornado disappears.

Dust devils

In the scorching heat of the desert it appears like a ghost, a pale, writhing column reaching to the sky. At first it is alone, but then another rises from the ground, and another. They are individuals, no two quite alike. There are fat ones and thin ones, tall ones and short ones, and all of them move unpredictably, wandering hither and thither as though searching for something lost. They rise, screaming yet insubstantial, then each vanishes as suddenly as it appeared until, eventually and for no apparent reason, all of them are gone. While they remain they seem to hunt and anything they capture they try to destroy. They are angry and very strong. Tents and flimsy buildings may not withstand them. They will tear doors from their hinges. They can kill people and livestock.

This, rather than the tornado, is the true whirlwind, familiar throughout history to all those who live in deserts or on the dry plains, and it is mysterious. God spoke to the prophet Job out of the whirlwind (Job 38:1), which, Job said, comes from the south; from where he lived that is the direction of the desert, although he does not mention it. In the many Old Testament references to whirlwinds they are described as fierce, terrible destroyers. Armies descend on their foes like a whirlwind and the whirlwind sweeps away everything in its path. It was the prophet Hosea who famously

Figure 23: *Dust devil.*
(National Center for
Atmospheric Research,
Boulder, CO)

warned idolaters and the impious that "they have sown the wind,
and they shall reap the whirlwind" (Hosea 8:7).

Its awesome reputation is not surprising. A tornado gives warning
of its approach. No one can miss the vast, dark cloud that heralds
most tornadoes (although some storm clouds are pale and indis-
tinct). Dust devils, on the other hand, are whirlwinds that spring
from nowhere. There is no cloud to generate them. They appear
suddenly beneath a clear, blue sky, with no warning, as towers of
furiously swirling dirt and air, sometimes reaching to a great height.
Nor do they appear alone. Where there is one, usually there will be

more and sometimes a small army of them may advance, as though living up to the biblical descriptions.

A whirlwind looks very like a tornado, but in fact it is not a tornado at all in the strict sense. A dust devil grows from the bottom up, rather than from the top down as a tornado does, and it is dust particles, not water droplets, which make it visible. There are other differences. Not every tornado grows from a mesocyclone. Waterspouts and landspouts, for example, often form in clouds that contain no mesocyclone or supercell (see page 76). Dust devils do not even need a parent cloud. If a tornado seems to hang beneath a cloud, because it forms in cloudless conditions a dust devil looks like a freestanding variety of tornado. It is as though the earth itself becomes alive and rises, howling.

It is obvious, when you think about it, that tornadoes and dust devils must form in different ways. A tornado is part of the huge cumulonimbus cloud from which it descends. The cloud grows because its upcurrents are driven by convection due partly to the latent heat released by the condensation of water vapor. They are partly powered by water and a full-size storm cloud holds up to half a million tons of water, its "fuel." Dust devils occur only in deserts and other very dry places. All air contains some water vapor, even over the driest desert where rain never falls, but tornadoes need moist ground to supply water that evaporates from the surface. This is something no desert can provide in anything like the amount required. Water plays no part in the life of the whirlwind.

Whirlwinds and tornadoes are different, but they have similarities. Both are caused by convection.

If ever you have tried to walk barefoot across sand or bare rock in the afternoon of a really blazing summer day, you know that the ground can be very hot. It can be so hot that walking is impossible and the only way to avoid being burned is to run fast. You do not pause anywhere until you reach a cool spot and the fact that all the bare ground exposed directly to the heat of the Sun is hot enough to hurt your feet may lead you to assume the ground is at the same temperature everywhere. It is not. Some surfaces reflect more heat than others and some materials conduct more heat than others downward, to lower levels, so removing it from the surface. Sand and different types of rock vary widely in this respect.

Movies and TV programs may give the impression that in a desert the ground surface is everywhere the same. The Sahara, for example, is an endless sea of sand dunes. True, a large area of it is like this, but most of the Sahara is not. The ground is stony and there is not much sand.

During the day, the Sun heats the ground and its temperature rises. It does not rise at the same rate everywhere, however, nor does it reach the same maximum temperature. In the central Sahara, sand, which reflects 75% more solar heat than rock, reaches a peak temperature of about 145° F around noon. Sandstone and basalt rock both reach a peak temperature of about 175° F at about 2 P.M. By that time the sand is starting to cool rapidly, but the rock does not start to cool until around 5 P.M. The surfaces all cool differently, too. By about 6 A.M., when the temperature is at its lowest, sand is at about 80° F, basalt at 100° F, and sandstone at 110° F. In California, granite rock surfaces can reach 125° F at noon, but by 6 P.M. they have cooled to 72° F.

Above ground, the air is much cooler. Two feet above a surface that heats to a maximum of 135° F air temperature through the day ranges between about 65° F and 85° F. Wind speed two feet above the ground also varies through the day, from about 2 MPH in the early morning to 18 MPH at noon.

Deserts are usually windy places, but sometimes there is a calm day and that is when whirlwinds may appear. Wind blowing across the surface mixes the air and cools the ground, two things whirl-winds cannot endure.

As the Sun rises the ground starts to heat and by early afternoon it has reached the highest temperature it will attain. Because the day is calm, with no wind to cool the ground, the surface is very hot, but it is markedly hotter in some places than in others. Patches of bare rock are about 30° F hotter than nearby sand dunes.

Air in contact with the surface is warmed by it. It expands and becomes less dense as it warms and so it rises through the cooler, denser air above it. Over the rock patches, however, air rises faster than it does over the sand because it is hotter. The expansion of the air reduces the surface air pressure everywhere, but pressure falls faster and lower over the rock than over the sand.

Some of the air over the sand dunes starts flowing toward the rock patches, where the atmospheric pressure is lower. The differ-ence in pressure is very small indeed, but it is enough to set up a flow of air. When it comes close to a rock patch, the inflowing air is warmed by the rock and joins the rising air current.

Its own vorticity makes the moving air begin to turn and, because it is converging toward a center of low pressure, in the northern hemisphere it turns counterclockwise. Air is now spiraling into the low-pressure region and then rising, still in a spiral. As it spirals inward, its speed increases to conserve its angular momen-tum (see page 48).

The ground is very dry, which means that individual sand and dust particles are not sticking to one another. Quite a light wind is sufficient to lift them. A wind of 12 MPH will move medium-size sand grains (about one-thousandth of an inch in diameter), and dust particles, which are much smaller than this, are raised even more easily. The smallest particles are carried upward in the spiraling vortex, along with leaves and any other loose material light enough to be lifted. It is these particles that make the whirlwind visible.

Figure 24: *Dust devil in Cordell, Oklahoma, May 22, 1981.* (National Severe Storm Laboratory, NOAA)

The size of the whirlwind and the strength of the wind around its center depend on the difference in air pressure inside and outside its core. This depends, in its turn, on the difference in temperature between different surfaces. There are often many different types of surface within a fairly small area, so the temperature differences vary from place to place.

Without warning, a whirlwind rises from a spot where the ground is especially hot. Then another appears not far away, over its own hot patch. When conditions are right for one whirlwind to rise they are usually right for a whole group of them. Most reach a height of about 100 feet, some rise to 300 feet. Really fierce ones, with winds powerful enough to do real damage, may be giants more than 6,000 feet tall.

Whirlwinds share with tornadoes their formation by convection, but there is no condensation to sustain them and no high-level wind shear to disperse the rising air and draw more from below. The supercell that produces tornadoes has about 10,000 times more energy than a dust devil.

As it rises, the hot air carries heat away from the ground, cooling it. After a time what had been a hot patch is at much the same temperature as its surroundings. Air pressure above it rises and air ceases to flow toward it. The dust devil dies.

How long this takes depends on the vigor of the original convection currents. Many dust devils last no more than seconds, but the strongest can survive for several hours.

Waterspouts

Everyone has heard of the Loch Ness monster. According to legend, the first person to have reported seeing it was St. Columba, in the year 565, when he forbade it from harming a person swimming in the loch. Since then thousands of people have described sightings of what they took to be "Nessie." If there has only ever been one monster, by now it is rather elderly, but remarkably fit for its age. It continues to appear and the stories about it have attracted millions of visitors to the loch and given rise to a thriving souvenir industry. You can buy "Nessie" models and toys in gift shops throughout Scotland.

Loch Ness is about 23 miles long, a little more than one mile wide, and its waters, 750 feet deep, are stained almost black by peat washed into it from the hills on either side. It is mysterious, often gloomy, and provides an entirely suitable home for a mythical monster. The loch is not unique, however. Almost every large lake in the world is said to harbor a monster of its own and monsters are alleged to inhabit several other Scottish lochs, although none has been searched for so thoroughly as the one in Loch Ness. Despite the searches, some of which involved the use of submersibles and one which comprised a full sonar scan by a fleet of boats sailing in formation, no persuasive evidence has been found for the existence of any large, unidentified animal. Nor has any physical evidence ever been found of this or the other lake monsters. There have been no bones, no skin, not even any otherwise inexplicable tracks left in soft mud.

Many possible explanations of the sightings have been offered and one of them is that "Nessie" is no more than an unusual movement of the water itself, produced entirely by a freak of the weather. If this is correct and the "monster" consists only of water, when it subsides, or "submerges," it leaves not the slightest trace. The suggestion is that at least some of the sightings may have been of "water devils." These cannot account for all the sightings, however, and while it is extremely unlikely that some unknown animal lurks in the depths of this or any other freshwater lake, it is not altogether impossible.

Water devils are the aquatic cousins of dust devils, but smaller and less violent. They may form by convection, but over certain lakes there is another mechanism capable of producing them. A suitable lake must be bounded by steep, high cliffs on one side and by low cliffs on another. When a strong wind blows over the low cliffs, across the water surface, and into the high cliffs, air may be deflected along and down the face of the high cliffs and back over the lake as a stream of air flowing in a different direction from the main wind. Somewhere over the lake the two streams may meet and the resulting wind shear may start the deflected air rotating. A combination of vorticity and the conservation of its angular momentum may then be sufficient to produce a vortex. As figure 25 suggests, the vortex is produced by eddying similar to that which occurs between buildings lining city streets, but on a larger scale.

The vortex is made visible by the water droplets it carries. Those near the base are whipped up from the surface into a small cloud. Those higher up are produced by condensation as moist air is drawn into the spiral, where the pressure is reduced. In this case, the fall

Figure 25: *Eddy vortex due to wind deflection.*

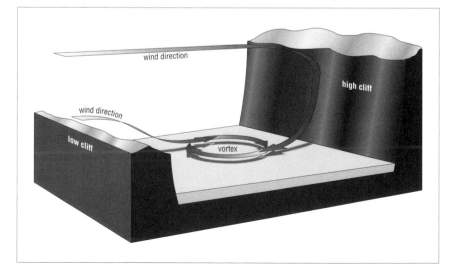

in pressure is not due to uneven heating of the surface and convection, but entirely to the Bernoulli effect (see box on page 117).

There are many lakes over which water devils may form. How often they occur depends on the frequency with which the wind blows from the right direction with sufficient force, but they are freak events and always unexpected. It is not hard to imagine that, seen from a distance, one might be mistaken for the long neck of an unknown animal, the cloud of spray and foam at its base suggesting a bulky body just below the surface. If you think you see a lake monster, look at the base of its "neck." If the water is frothing and bubbling, probably it is a water devil, its "body" composed of water whipped up by air flowing into the spiral.

Most water devils are small and not especially dangerous, but there are exceptions and even mild ones can be frightening. A party of anglers is said to have met one in February 1978 on Loch Dionard, in the mountains many miles north of Loch Ness. A rising wind had made them decide to head for the shore when they heard a strange noise behind them and turned. What they saw was a swirling column of water, about 10 feet high, close and heading straight for them. As it passed over them it lifted their boat from the water, spun it around, then dropped it. The water devil continued across the loch, then died and disappeared.

Water devils resemble waterspouts, but these are very much bigger and it is convection that causes them, not eddies in a horizontal wind flow. They can occur anywhere, but are most often seen over warm water. Sometimes one forms over a very large lake, but most form over the sea. They are fairly common in the Caribbean and off the Florida Keys. Professor Howard B. Bluestein, a leading authority on tornadoes, records that in 1975 he was almost late for his own presentation at a conference on tropical meteorology at Key Biscayne because he was gazing enraptured at a group of waterspouts dancing outside his hotel.

Some waterspouts are true tornadoes, hanging beneath a cumulonimbus cloud that contains a mesocyclone. If the cloud drifts out over the sea, the tornado will turn into a waterspout. The only difference between a waterspout of this kind and a tornado over land is that while it crosses water there is no dust and other solid material to be drawn into the vortex. Instead, water is swept up and forms a swirling cloud called a *spray ring*, around the base, and no matter what its color may have been over land, when it becomes a waterspout it will turn white because its funnel consists of only water.

A waterspout that is a true tornado can be powerful, and if it moves back over land, it can cause a great deal of damage. In 1935, a tornado at Norfolk, Virginia, moved over the sea, where it destroyed part of a pier and threw small boats onto the shore. Then

Figure 26: *Waterspout off port bow of the USS F. D. Roosevelt on October 5, 1962.* (Naval Photographic Center, U.S. Navy)

it moved back to start wrecking the town, demolishing several buildings before it died.

Waterspouts can form without the help of a mesocyclone. These are generally weaker than tornado waterspouts. Most are less than about 300 feet in diameter at the base and generate winds of no more than 50 MPH. You are most likely to see a waterspout of this kind over shallow water on a hot day. In deep water, there is usually enough mixing between the surface layer that is warmed by the Sun and cooler water below to prevent the water reaching a sufficiently high temperature. Shallow water, which can be heated all the way to the sea or lake bed, grows warmer than deep water. This explains why waterspouts are often seen close to the shore, especially in sheltered bays.

The high surface temperature warms the air in contact with it and causes strong convection upcurrents. These are very moist because a large amount of water evaporates into the warm air. As the air rises, it cools adiabatically (see box on page 26), water vapor condenses, and cumulus clouds develop. If the air is sufficiently unstable, inflowing air can start to rotate, and it is this which grows into the waterspout.

Watch a waterspout, or look at a photograph of one, and you might well suppose that it sucks water from below and carries it into the cloud in its upcurrents, rather like a vacuum cleaner. This is what your common sense might tell you, but it would be wrong. Except for the water in the spray ring at the base, which is whipped up from the surface, the funnel consists entirely of droplets that have condensed due to the drop in pressure as air spirals inward. It is fresh water, even if the waterspout is over the sea, although it might contain some salt, because some spray droplets at the base evaporate, leaving solid salt crystals which are swept upward and dissolve as water vapor condenses onto them.

It is not only waterspouts, water devils, and dust devils that can form in the absence of a mesocyclone. Professor Bluestein has described how, in 1981, he was hunting tornadoes in Texas when he saw a tornado behind the car in which he was a passenger. He reported it to colleagues at the National Severe Storms Laboratory, in Norman, Oklahoma. They examined it with their radar and found, to their surprise, that the tornado was beneath a fairly weak storm cloud that was still developing and contained no mesocyclone. It closely resembled a waterspout that had developed over land. Some scientists call tornadoes of this kind *nonsupercell tornadoes*. Professor Bluestein calls them *landspouts*.

They are something of a mystery. Meteorologists can explain tornadoes that develop from mesocyclones in supercells, but the fact that a tornado can also occur without a mesocyclone to start it rotating suggests the usual explanation is incomplete.

Other small tornadoes sometimes form in the gust front where the downcurrents spill out beneath a supercell. These often rotate anticyclonically (clockwise in the northern hemisphere), because they spin in diverging air. They are called *gustnadoes*.

Raining fish

When it rains very heavily, we often say it is raining "cats and dogs." Some people believe this expression is a corruption of *catedupe*, an old French word for "waterfall", but cats have often been associated with rain and at one time people in many different parts of the world used to believe they could influence the weather. In parts of Java, people used to bathe two cats, one male and one female, when they wanted rain. In Europe, witches were supposed to take the form of a cat when they rode on storms, and in Scotland they were believed to raise sea storms with the help of cats. Probably this belief arose from Norse mythology, in which the world serpent, lying at the bottom of the sea, sometimes takes the form of a cat. Dogs and wolves were associated with the wind and with the god Odin. Together, cats and dogs symbolize heavy rain and strong winds.

Whatever the origin of the phrase may be, no one supposes that cats and dogs can really fall from the sky. The very idea of such a thing is clearly absurd. On the other hand, about a century ago the Irish writer and historian Patrick Weston Joyce included a strange story in his book *The Wonders of Ireland*. Like much of his book, it was taken from an early work called *Chronica Scotorum*. The event took place on the feast day of St. George in 1055 at Rosdalla, near Kilbeggan, today a small town about 50 miles west of Dublin. As Joyce retells it, the people of Rosdalla saw "a great steeple of fire, in the exact shape of a circular belfry, or what we now call a round tower. For nine hours it remained there in sight of all: and during the whole time, flocks of large dark-colored birds without number kept flying in and out through the doors and windows. . . Sometimes a number of them would swoop suddenly down, and snatch up in their talons dogs, cats or any other small animal that happened to lie in their way; and when they had risen again to a great height they would drop them dead to the ground."

Unless the story is entirely invented, this was a tornado. Observers have often likened tornadoes to steeples or towers, and they can look as though they are made of fire if lightning or some other electrical phenomenon illuminates them from inside. Debris swept swirling aloft by a tornado can look like a flock of birds. This is not the only time such a comparison has been made, although nowadays people usually know what it is they are watching. It was clearly a powerful tornado, for it lasted a remarkably long time. Did it snatch up dogs and cats "in its talons," raise them to a great height, then drop them dead? It may well have done so, and the event was already so extraordinary it is hard to see why anyone would want to embellish it. If we believe the main claim, that a tornado struck Rosdalla in 1055, which is certainly believable, there seems no good reason to doubt the rest of the story. It appears, therefore, that on at least one occasion it has "rained cats and dogs," even if there were not very many of them and they were dead when they landed.

It can hardly be called "rain," but on May 17, 1983, a few sheep may have traveled by air to a field at Baileyhaulwen, in Powys, Wales. They came from another field several hundred feet away and the farmer who found them said they could not possibly have reached his field on foot. To do so, he said, they would have had to cross a river and stone walls.

We can imagine some dreadful disaster that kills birds, causing large numbers of them to fall to the ground, but we do not expect other animals to drop from the sky. Other animals, after all, have no business being in the sky in the first place. Yet it happens.

In 1666, on the Wednesday before Easter, there was a fall near the town of Wrotham, in Kent, England, of small fishes about the length of a man's little finger. They were judged to be young whiting. Rather more fish fell at Mountain Ash, Glamorgan, Wales, on February 9, 1859. On this occasion there were two showers of them, each lasting about two minutes and with 10 minutes between showers, and the fish, mainly minnows and sticklebacks, covered an area of 80 yards by 12, or 8,640 square feet. Fish continue to fall. Flounders and Dover sole fell on East Ham, London, in May 1984, but such falls are not confined to Britain. On the morning of October 23, 1947, A. D. Bajkov, a biologist who worked for the U.S. Department of Wildlife and Fisheries, was eating breakfast with his wife in a restaurant in Marksville, Louisiana, when the waitress told them fish were falling from the sky into the trees. "We went immediately to collect some of the fish . . . They were freshwater fish native to local waters: large-mouthed black bass, goggle-eye, and hickory shad." He said the individual fishes were two to nine inches long.

Sometimes the weather delivers shellfish. On May 28, 1881, periwinkles fell on Worcester, England. These are edible mollusks, up to one inch long, and they live among rocks and seaweed on rocky shores. Worcester is more than 50 miles from the nearest seashore. Thirsk, in Yorkshire, is only 25 miles from the sea. It also received a fall of winkles, in June 1984, this time accompanied by a starfish (which is not edible). Pond mussels fell on Paderborn, Germany, in 1892; snails fell on Chester, Pennsylvania, in 1870 and on Algiers in 1973; jellyfish fell on Bath, England, in 1894; and in 1954 crayfish landed on parts of Florida.

Frogs drop from the sky more often than fish, however, sometimes in very large quantities. On June 12, 1954, for example, Sylvia Mowday was with her two young children in a park at Sutton Coldfield, on the north side of Birmingham, England, when the sky clouded over and it started to rain heavily. They ran for shelter and watched what Mrs. Mowday thought was soft hail, until Timothy, her 11-year-old son, said, "It isn't hail, Mum, they're frogs, baby frogs," and so they were. Mrs. Mowday said they were "coming down like snowflakes." Frogs have also fallen on Arkansas, on January 2, 1973, on Southgate, London, on August 17, 1977, in Greece in 1991, and on September 24, 1973 toads fell at Brignoles, France.

Nor are these the only remarkable things to fall to the ground. Hazelnuts fell on Bristol, England, on March 13, 1977, and in 1979 plant seeds and beans fell in Southampton, England.

There are far too many of these stories for them to be hoaxes. The most likely explanation is that tornadoes cause them. Consider the account given by Mrs. Mowday. She and her children ran for shelter because the sky clouded over and it started to rain heavily. Until then it had been a fine summer day, just the day on which the air might have been very unstable. If it was a towering cumulonimbus cloud that produced the rain, the cloud may have contained a mesocyclone. There could have been a tornado nearby. Had the tornado crossed a pond—and there is a large lake in that park—perhaps it could have caught up young frogs, only recently grown from polliwogs and emerging onto a bank that the rain had made wet.

The funnel of a tornado or waterspout is visible because water vapor has condensed in it, not because of water raised from the surface, but powerful vortices can and do pick up all kinds of objects and sometimes water. The 1935 tornado at Norfolk, Virginia, crossed a creek, removing all the water and some mud from the bed. The water would have merged with that in the cloud and fallen again as rain, mixed with the mud, and neither water nor mud would have been noticed when they fell. Had it picked up fish or frogs, on the other hand, their fall would have been noticed.

When strange objects fall from the sky the event is bound to be reported, especially if those objects are animals, and the fall must always seem mysterious. So far as the people who observe the falls are concerned, there is no obvious explanation. Tornadoes often occur in remote, rural areas and go unnoticed. In any case, they will usually have disappeared by the time their parent cloud crosses an inhabited area and its upcurrents are no longer powerful enough to keep aloft whatever items they have collected.

Some puzzles remain, however. If a tornado picks up fish or frogs, why does it pick up nothing else? Gravel never seems to fall from the sky, for example, yet it is plentiful on the banks and beds of rivers and ponds. When they are wet, do the individual stones stick to one another too tightly to be lifted? Pond plants never seem to be dropped, either. Some water plants are rooted securely, but others float clear of the bottom, so why do tornadoes leave them behind? It is also odd that fish and frogs seem to fall all together. Most tornado debris ends up scattered over a wide area.

These are questions that so far have no answers. There can be no doubt that frogs, fish, and other items do fall from the sky. They have been doing so throughout history, the falls continue to this day, and too many people have seen them for the phenomenon to be dismissed. It does happen and tornadoes are the most likely cause. That certain features of these events remain unexplained does not mean something other than tornadoes and waterspouts causes them, but only that scientists still have a great deal to learn about what goes on inside mesocyclones and the vortices that descend from them.

When and where tornadoes happen

Tornadoes occur far more frequently in the United States than in any other country (see page 85), but tornadic storms are by no means confined to North America. Europe has experienced many (see page 89) and cyclones moving north from the Bay of Bengal often bring them to the eastern part of the Indian subcontinent. Bangladesh suffered three in 1991, for example, one in April and two, a couple of days apart, in May. In 1993, there was one tornado in Bangladesh in January and another in West Bengal in April. Few are reported from Africa, but this may be the only continent to escape them and even its apparent freedom may be due to lack of reports, rather than lack of tornadoes. There is no obvious reason why tornadoes should not occur in those parts of Africa where the climate is not too dry for them. Much of Australia is desert, but about 15 tornadoes are reported there each year and the true number may be considerably greater because the country is so sparsely populated away from the cities.

It may be no more than a coincidence, but Africa also escapes hurricanes. Most Atlantic hurricanes begin as tropical thunderstorms over Africa. The storms create an atmospheric disturbance that moves westward, over the ocean, and produces a "kink" in the prevailing airflow, called an "easterly wave" (because it begins in the east). Easterly waves can intensify to produce small areas of low atmospheric pressure, and if these grow and intensify further they turn into tropical depressions. These can dissipate, but if they develop, they become tropical storms and then, when their winds exceed 75 MPH, the qualifying minimum, they become hurricanes. Hurricanes move from east to west in the tropical Atlantic and Caribbean. The huge storm clouds that produce hurricanes also trigger tornadoes.

What are called "hurricanes" in the Atlantic and Caribbean are known as "cyclones" in the Bay of Bengal and "typhoons" in the Pacific. These are just different names for the same kind of storm, and several more are used locally in various parts of the world. The technical name for them, which meteorologists use, is "tropical cyclones." No matter what people call them, they are huge, fierce storms, and tornadoes are often associated with them. Any region that experiences tropical cyclones can expect tornadoes. Tropical cyclones occur in Madagascar, but are rare over the continent of Africa, although some are recorded. There was a hurricane in Algeria on January 15, 1922, for example. Absence of tropical cyclones brings no guarantee that tornadoes will not strike, however, only that the absence of one of their causes may make them rather less frequent.

What are known locally as "tornadoes" are common in the countries of West Africa south of the Sahara. They occur most frequently at the beginning and end of the rainy season, from March to May and in October and November near the coast and from May to September inland. In fact, they are line squalls (see page 24) that travel from east to west, sometimes for as much as 500 miles, at about 30 MPH. They bring violent thunderstorms and at the gust front, where downcurrents spill outward from the storm cloud, winds can reach 80 MPH inland, although they seldom exceed 40 MPH near the coast. The winds raise large amounts of dust and when the gust front passes there is often, but not always, torrential rain.

In drier regions, dust devils (whirlwinds) are common. The biggest of these, called "haboobs" (from the Arabic word for "wind"), form along fronts, often about 15 miles long and moving at about 35 MPH. Haboobs are whirlwinds, but their winds seldom exceed about 30 MPH, except in gusts. The dust they carry penetrates everything, making them a serious nuisance, but haboobs are much gentler than full-scale tornadoes.

Tropical cyclones occur exclusively in the tropics, but they are only one cause of tornadoes. Countries outside the tropics also experience twisters and Africa should receive its share, even if we do not get to hear about them.

Three conditions are necessary to trigger tornadoes. Moist air must be very unstable, towering cumulonimbus storm clouds must form in the unstable air, and the high-level wind must blow at a different direction from the wind at lower levels to provide the wind shear that removes rising air. All of these conditions are common and it is not unusual for all three to coincide. This does not mean there will be tornadoes, but it does mean they are possible.

Strong but uneven heating of moist ground will make the air unstable. Air is warmed by contact with the ground and water vapor evaporates into it. The warm, moist air expands, rises, and starts to cool adiabatically (see box on page 26). This makes some of its water vapor condense, releasing latent heat and sustaining the instability. This is the way summer thunderstorms develop in temperate climates, and in the tropics and subtropics such storms are much commoner and usually bigger. Because the instability that triggers them is caused by heating of the ground surface, storms of this kind are most likely to occur in the late afternoon and early evening, when the ground has been warming for several hours, but has not yet started to cool. In the United States, the number of tornadoes reaches a maximum between May and September. Two-thirds of all tornadoes occur between 2 P.M. and 8 P.M., and about one tornado in four occurs between 4 P.M. and 6 P.M. Tornadoes are least likely to form around dawn, when the air is at its most stable. This suggests that many tornadoes are linked to isolated thunderstorms.

In the world as a whole, there are about 1,800 thunderstorms happening at any one time, and every day there are something like 45,000. Not all of them are caused by uneven heating of the ground.

Anything that forces moist air to rise will render it unstable if it is raised higher than its condensation level, at which its temperature falls low enough for water vapor to condense, and if it is moist enough to release significant amounts of latent heat. An air mass

Figure 27. *University of Oklahoma graduate students probing a tornado near Hodges, Texas, with a portable Doppler radar on May 13, 1989.* (Copyright Howard B. Bluestein)

that has crossed the ocean will be moist when it reaches land, and if it is forced over a mountain range it may well become sufficiently unstable for cumulonimbus storm clouds to form in it. Storm clouds may also develop along a front where warm, moist air is undercut by advancing colder, denser air. Frontal storm clouds of this kind can merge into squall lines, which often trigger tornado outbreaks.

Air masses move throughout the year, but vigorous frontal systems form only where differences in the characteristics of the two air masses is fairly extreme. Fronts are commonest where polar and Arctic air meet tropical air. This happens in eastern North America, in winter as far south as the Gulf of Mexico, in northwest Europe, and in east Asia. In winter it also happens in a belt between the eastern Mediterranean and Caspian Seas.

Thunderstorms may develop along fronts at any time of year and some of them may be powerful enough to trigger tornadoes. This means that while spring and summer are the most likely seasons for tornadoes, they can also occur in fall and winter. Just as no part of the world is immune, neither is any time of year.

Whether or not tornadoes will form depends on the third necessary factor. There must be wind shear aloft, to disperse the air that rises by convection in the upcurrents. Fronts can supply wind shear, but often it is the jet stream that does so (see page 16). This moves with the seasons and its location at any particular time provides a clue to the places where tornadoes are most likely.

In summer, the Polar Front Jet Stream lies across North America in the latitude of the Great Lakes, passes over Europe just to the south of Britain, and continues across central Asia. In winter it is farther south and blows much faster. It crosses North America along a line from approximately the southern tip of Baja California to Chesapeake Bay. On the other side of the Atlantic it lies across the Sahara, continuing over Asia just to the north of the Indian subcontinent. In spring and fall it is moving between its summer and winter positions. These are its average locations, however, and on a shorter time scale the jet stream is quite variable in its direction and force, from time to time briefly disappearing altogether.

Add these factors together and a pattern emerges. Strong convection in moist, unstable air, with wind shear aloft, can occur almost anywhere at almost any time, but it is a little more likely in some places and at some times than others.

Isolated storms vigorous enough to send upcurrents all the way across the jet stream and into the lower stratosphere are more frequent in summer than in winter. They require strong surface heating to trigger them. The season for tropical cyclones begins in late summer and continues into the fall. These too require high-level wind shear and produce towering cumulonimbus clouds in which supercells can develop and they are associated with tornadoes.

There are, therefore, two reasons why tornadoes are more frequent in summer than at other seasons.

Tropical cyclones form in the tropics, but often move into higher latitudes. Tornadoes are likely to be more frequent along the tracks tropical cyclones usually follow than they are elsewhere.

Tornadoes may also be expected below the jet stream. Its position varies, but on any particular day during summer its location indicates where tornadoes may occur. Fast-moving cold fronts may also generate tornadic storms along squall lines. The speed of the front provides the best clue to the likelihood of tornadoes, because the faster the cold air advances, the faster it lifts the warm air ahead of it, and the more rapidly warm air is made to rise, the more unstable it is likely to become.

These are no more than very general indications, however. Tornadoes can be expected whenever and wherever the conditions needed to trigger them are met, but it does not follow that they will occur. Nowadays they can often be predicted (see page 101), but only by the presence of their parent mesocyclones and, since these are short-lived, by the time a warning can be given the danger is already very close. Tornadoes appear and disappear abruptly and break every rule by which scientists try to explain their behavior.

Tornado Alley

The United States suffers far more tornadoes than any other country in the world. On average, there are 800 every year, and they kill 80 people and injure 1,500. There are good years and bad ones. 1963 was a good year, with only about 450 tornadoes, but in 1992, which was a very bad one, there were 1,300. In May of most years, which is a peak month in all states, there may be five tornadoes a day.

As the map in figure 28 shows, however, American tornadoes are not distributed at all evenly. States vary greatly in area, so the best way to count tornadoes is as the average number each year for every 10,000 square miles of territory. This way of counting makes it possible to compare the importance of tornadoes in geographically small states, such as Hawaii and Connecticut, with that in large states, like Texas and California.

No tornado has ever been reported in Alaska. This is not surprising, because of the climate, but Alaska is the only state to escape tornadoes completely. There is an average of at least one each year in every other state, but they are much rarer in the western states than in the east and south. They are also uncommon in

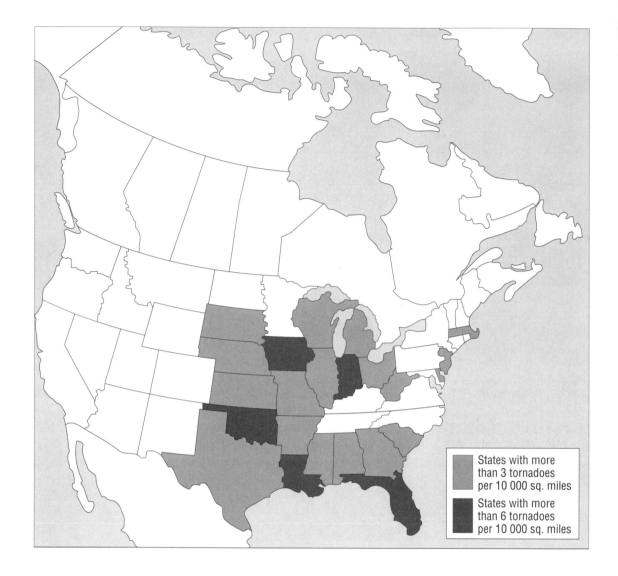

Figure 28: *Frequency of tornadoes in the United States: Average number per year, 1961–1990.*

Hawaii, which averages 1.55 tornadoes a year for every 10,000 square miles of territory.

To some extent they may be underreported in the more sparsely populated western states, but the extent of this is probably not very important. There may be dust devils, but true tornadoes cannot form in deserts or regions where the climate is dry because there is insufficient surface moisture to sustain the violent convection currents needed for a mesocyclone to form. In any case, most of California is not sparsely populated, yet it experiences annually only 0.26 tornadoes for every 10,000 of its square miles.

Kansas, on the other hand, where the most famous of all fictional tornadoes carried away Dorothy and her dog, Toto, in *The Wonder-*

ful Wizard of Oz, averages 4.65 tornadoes a year for every 10,000 square miles. For the state as a whole, this works out at 36 tornadoes a year. Despite its tornado-prone reputation, however, which was created by *The Wonderful Wizard of Oz*, Kansas is far from being the most sorely afflicted state. You are much more likely to see a tornado to the south, in Oklahoma. That state suffers an average of 47 a year, or 6.85 for every 10,000 square miles, and they are almost as frequent in Louisiana, Indiana, and Iowa. Florida is the most dangerous place of all. It has an average of 52 tornadoes a year, or 9.59 per 10,000 square miles.

Tornadoes are rare to the west of the Rocky Mountains and north of latitude 45°, but there are ten states in which they are fairly common: Alabama, Arkansas, Florida, Iowa, Kansas, Mississippi, Missouri, Nebraska, Oklahoma, and Texas. In the southern states the monthly number of tornadoes peaks between March and May with a second peak in November. In the northern states most tornadoes are a little later, between April and June, and there is no second peak in the fall.

All of these ten states lie to the east of a line running from Nebraska to Texas. This line also marks the boundary of the Great Plains, with land to the west rising into the Rocky Mountains. The weather systems that generate tornadoes develop over the Great Plains and the area most severely affected by them is often known as "Tornado Alley."

This is where the major tornado outbreaks occur. The 1925 outbreak of possibly seven tornadoes began in Missouri and crossed Illinois and Indiana. Of a total of 11 states affected by an outbreak in May 1973, Alabama and Arkansas were so ravaged by tornadoes they were declared disaster areas. The Super Outbreak of 148 tornadoes in April of the following year struck all the states between Michigan and Alabama and there was another outbreak in June of the same year in Oklahoma, Kansas, and Arkansas. A tornado destroyed a shopping mall in Mississippi on January 10, 1975; and in April 1977 there was a major outbreak in West Virginia, Virginia, Alabama, Mississippi, Georgia, Tennessee, and Kentucky. A single tornado, but one that killed 59 people in Wichita Falls, moved through the Red River Valley, on the border between Texas and Oklahoma, in April 1979. Year after year the story continues. In November 1992 an outbreak of up to 45 tornadoes struck 11 states from Texas to Ohio, in March 1994 there was an outbreak in Alabama, Georgia, the Carolinas, and Tennessee, and on January 23, 1996, the state governor declared a state of emergency in Shreveport, Louisiana, after a tornado had damaged about 200 buildings and injured 30 residents of a nursing home. One eyewitness reported that "the trees were bouncing around . . . trees a couple of hundred feet tall, they were absolutely tossing around like crazy."

It is because of its geography that the United States suffers so badly from tornadoes. Compare North America with Russia and it becomes clear why this is so. Both are large continental areas in latitudes between the Arctic and about 25° N at the tip of Florida and about 35° N at the southern shore of the Caspian Sea, and both are about the same size (the United States and Canada together cover about 7.4 million square miles and Russia covers about 6.6 million square miles). Both have a large plain, but in North America this occupies only the eastern half of the continent. To its west the land rises steadily toward the high peaks of the Rocky Mountains. Russia has no comparable north-to-south mountain range in the west to affect the inflow of maritime air, and its plain covers most of the country. North America is surrounded by sea, but Russia is bounded by Europe to the west and by the Asian landmass to the south.

In winter, the Russian landmass cools rapidly and a great mass of dense air subsides over it. This air mass is very stable and produces a region of high pressure (an anticyclone) covering most of the country. A pressure of 1,076 millibars once measured at Irkutsk is believed to be the highest atmospheric pressure ever recorded anywhere. Weather systems moving from west to east are pushed to the north, over Scandinavia, or south, over the Mediterranean, by air spilling outward from the anticyclone. In summer, the pattern reverses. The land warms rapidly and pressure falls until the winter anticyclone is replaced by an equally large area of low pressure. This draws in air from surrounding regions. Atlantic air masses bring rain in summer and have some warming effect in winter over the western part of the country, but in general pressure gradients are shallow and the climate is very stable.

Any large continental plain is likely to experience tornadoes and Russia is no exception. Tornadoes are well known there, especially in the south, where uneven heating of the ground generates strong convection leading to powerful thunderstorms. North America is different because it is exposed to a much greater variety of air masses.

Maritime polar air masses (see box on page 4) form over the North Pacific and move eastward. As it crosses the Rockies the cool, moist air cools further and loses much of its moisture. Now fairly dry, the air sinks down the eastern slopes, but the descent is gentle, because high ground extends a long way to the east of the mountains. It warms a little during its descent, but by the time it reaches the plains it is still relatively dense and advances, fairly slowly, behind a weak cold front aligned approximately from southwest to northeast. The jet stream is similarly aligned directly above it.

Farther south, over Texas, New Mexico, and Mexico, continental tropical air masses form and move north. In spring and summer, as the land warms rapidly, they bring hot, dry air into the plains. At the same time, maritime tropical air masses are moving northwest from the Gulf of Mexico. This air is warm and moist, but the continental tropical air is warmer, so when they meet, over Mexico and the southern United States, the maritime air is held beneath the less dense continental air. It warms further as it crosses the hot land surface. Ordinarily, this would trigger strong convection and much of its water vapor would condense to form clouds, but the overlying layer of even warmer air prevents this. Only small clouds can form, and they are confined to the lower part of the atmosphere.

When this air reaches the western side of the Great Plains it meets the cold air moving down from the high ground. The cold air undercuts the warmer air. Now there is a "sandwich" made from air derived from three distinct air masses. At the base is maritime polar air that has lost much of its moisture, at the top is very dry, continental tropical air, and between them is very moist, maritime tropical air from the Gulf. As the warm, moist air is forced to rise up the advancing cold front it expands, cools adiabatically, water vapor starts to condense, and the change of temperature with height decreases from the dry to the saturated adiabatic lapse rate (see box on page 32). The air is unstable, and the front increases its instability by making it continue to rise. Now really big clouds form until the convection becomes so vigorous that upcurrents break through the overlying layer of continental tropical air and the cumulonimbus clouds tower all the way to the tropopause and sometimes across it.

These events produce the biggest, most violent thunderstorms in the world. Above them, aligned with the cold front, is the jet stream, which provides strong wind shear at high altitude. All the ingredients for creating mesocyclones are assembled and the tornadoes follow inevitably.

The "sandwiching" of air masses begins along the western boundary of the Great Plains and continues, usually in a south-easterly direction, with the advance of the cold front. This is what turns the region into "Tornado Alley" and it makes the United States unique. No such collision of air happens routinely anywhere else in the world. Tornadoes can and do strike anywhere and at any time, but it is because of this particular collision that they are so frequent on the eastern side of the United States.

Tornadoes in Europe

About 20 miles southwest of Bristol, England, is the village of Congresbury. There, at about breakfast time one January morning in 1991, people noticed a big, dark cloud approaching. Obviously, a storm was about to break out, but most people were busy getting ready for work or school and no one took much notice. Then suddenly, with no warning, tiles were being ripped from roofs, debris was flying everywhere, and a huge wind rushed through the houses. Moments later, when it had passed, power lines were down, trees were uprooted, homes were demolished. A tornado had passed through the village.

Europeans do not expect their weather to behave in this way. What they know of tornadoes they learn mainly from the American experience of them, and people tend to assume they are an exclusively American phenomenon. Indeed, many Europeans might dismiss stories of home-grown tornadoes as pure fantasy. Yet while it is true that tornadoes are much less common in Europe than in America and those that do occur are mild by comparison with their cousins across the ocean, Europe does not escape. No one can be sure how many there are, but estimates put the figure for Britain at between 30 and 60 in most years and a study over a 25-year period found there are an average of 10 a year in Italy.

Weather systems tend to reach western Europe from the Atlantic, with maritime air masses in which frontal systems and depressions develop. These encounter continental air masses farther east, which sometimes extend westward as anticyclones or ridges of high pressure. Storms often develop in summer and fall, when anticyclones bring clear skies and light winds, allowing strong convection currents above moist ground to produce cumulonimbus clouds. Nowhere in Europe, however, does the geography cause the kind of collision of air masses that brings such violent squall-line storms to the Great Plains of the United States. To the east, the European climate is continental, with hot summers and cold winters. In the west it is maritime, with rainfall distributed fairly evenly throughout the year, mild winters, and cool summers. This is not a type of climate capable of great violence except on rare occasions. Nevertheless, it can be affected by vigorous cold fronts and uneven summer heating, both of which can trigger thunderstorms powerful enough to trigger tornadoes.

Tornadoes do occur, and in Europe they can strike at any time of year and there is no season in which the likelihood of them increases. Some of the most severe, including that which caused a major disaster in Scotland in 1879 (see page 93), have happened in winter, but there is no pattern to their occurrence. Most pass unremarked, because they affect remote, rural areas and are gone before anyone sees them.

Occasionally, though, people are forced to take notice when they strike an important center of population. This happened in Russia on June 9 and 10, 1984, when an outbreak of tornadoes struck Ivanovo, Gorky, Kalinin, Kostroma, and Yaroslavl, five important towns. Hundreds of people were killed, trees were uprooted, and brick houses and factories were demolished.

On December 8, 1954, a Londoner described seeing a car fly past his shop window, 15 feet above the ground, and land upright without so much as bursting a tire. Its flight was caused by a tornado that could not be ignored. The twister struck west London during the afternoon rush hour and left a 9-mile track of devastation varying between 300 and 1,200 feet in width through Chiswick, Gunnersbury, Acton, Golders Green, and Southgate. The roof was torn from Gunnersbury train station and a factory in Acton was demolished. Fortunately, few people were injured and there were no deaths.

Doors and windows were blown out when a small tornado crossed the southern suburbs of Birmingham, England, in June 1937, and earlier still, tornadoes accompanied a cold front that crossed south Wales in October 1913. What were probably small tornadoes have been recorded as extremely violent but very local weather disturbances in many parts of England, especially in central and eastern regions, where the land is generally flat.

One of the most curious accounts of a tornadic storm concerns the church of St. Pancras, in the village of Widecombe-in-the-Moor, in Devon. The "moor" of the name is Dartmoor and Widecombe lies on its eastern side, about 20 miles northeast of Plymouth.

During the morning service on October 21, 1638, the church packed with worshippers, an event took place that was far beyond anything the villagers had ever experienced. The village schoolmaster recorded it in *A true Relation of most strange and lamentable accidents happening in the Parish Church of Wydecombe in Devonshire, on Sunday, the 21st of October 1638*. Hardly surprisingly, it was said to have left the church smelling of fire and brimstone. One of the pinnacles on the church tower was destroyed (it was replaced later) and the roof collapsed. The damage was caused by what is now thought to have been a tornado, but the twister did not arrive alone and it was its companion that savaged the congregation. The interior of the church was set ablaze in a way that "so affrighted the whole Congregation that the most part of them fell downe." The parson escaped injury, but according to the account, "the lightning seized upon his poor wife, fired her ruff, and linnen next to her body, and her clothes, to the burning of many parts of her body in a very pitiful manner". A parishioner, "adventuring to run out of the church, had her clothes set on fire, and was not only strangely burnt and scorched, but had her flesh torn about her back, almost to the very bones." In all, 62 people were injured and, according to different reports of the event, somewhere between five and 50 were killed. One of those was said to have died when his head was "rent into three pieces."

Tornadoes accompany severe thunderstorms but the companion to the 1638 tornado seems likely to have been an even rarer electrical phenomenon associated with such storms, a *fireball*. Little is known about fireballs except that they really happen and they can be very dangerous. There are descriptions of them from all over the world and they seem invariably to set fire to the first flammable material they touch, which would explain how clothes burst into flames at

Widecombe. In the modern world they also burn out electrical wiring, causing any appliance connected to a power supply to explode. In 1984, one fell through the ground in Leeds, Yorkshire, and set fire to a gas pipe, which exploded and burst a water main. At least two caused damage when violent thunderstorms crossed southern England on July 20, 1992. A house in Crawley, Sussex, burst into flames and in Dormansland, Surrey, a fireball was seen to descend and strike a house. Observers said it was like a large, red ball that fell from the sky. It made a hole six feet wide in the roof and started a fire in the loft and a bedroom. The storm was very fierce that night and there may well have been a tornado, although it caused no evident damage. Whatever they are, fireballs are not ordinary lightning. Nor are they ball lightning, the glowing spheres that float horizontally, passing through walls and windows. Ball lightning usually disappears suddenly with a loud pop.

Tornadoes and waterspouts move erratically over the surface and suction vortices that form around the center of a tornado sometimes leave behind a spiraling trail of flattened crops. When suction vortices form at all, usually there are several, but not always. There can be just one, which forms and then dissipates almost at once. During the few seconds that it lasts, the vortex may not have time to wander and instead of a spiraling trail it leaves behind an isolated swirl of leveled plants.

During the 1980s, Dr. Terence Meaden of the Tornado Research Organization proposed that brief, stationary vortices might be the cause of "crop circles." These were delighting journalists, attracting believers in flying saucers, and giving rise to extraordinary stories of strange lights in the sky and weird noises. At first, the circles themselves were circular areas of flattened crops inside fields growing cereals, with no track or footprints leading to them from the edges of the fields. They have been seen in Japan and other countries, but it was in southern England that they were most abundant. At their peak, several new ones were appearing every night during late summer, when the cereal crops were almost ripe enough for harvesting and the circles were clearly visible.

As the enthusiasm of the UFOlogists grew wilder, the circles started to become more elaborate. Circles had smaller circles around their edges, circles were linked by straight lines, and eventually crops were being laid flat in patterns resembling scientific formulae. The craze came to an end in September 1991, when two middle-aged men explained how they had been making the circles and other patterns, equipped with string, stepladders, and boards. They did it for fun, but there were far too many for the two of them to have been responsible for all the circles. There must have been other hoaxers and, besides the hoaxes, a few circles that were not hoaxes at all.

Some witnesses said they had watched as short-lived, stationary vortices flattened circles of vegetation. These were far short of full-scale tornadoes, but at least some may have formed as eddies, much like those that generate water devils on some lakes (see page 75). Eddy vortices are especially common on the lee side of high ground and once air starts spiraling, the conservation of its angular momentum tends to accelerate it toward the center.

Tornadoes of the past

Look at a map of Scotland, and you will see that just north of Edinburgh there is a wide estuary (or firth). This is the Firth of Forth and to its north lies the county of Fife. Fife, in turn, is bounded to the north by the Firth of Tay, with the city of Dundee on its northern shore. Roads and railroads linking Dundee and Edinburgh must either cross the two firths or make a long detour inland to cross the rivers further upstream, where they are narrower. In the last century, railroads were expanding rapidly to link every part of Britain and a bridge was built across the Forth. Then, on June 20, 1877, the north coast of Fife was linked to Dundee by another bridge, across the Tay.

In those days, engineers knew little about the effects of wind on bridges and the Tay Bridge was not stressed in the way all bridges have been since. Nevertheless, it was proudly boasted that the new bridge, a little over one mile long, was strong enough to withstand the worst weather imaginable.

On the evening of Sunday, December 28, 1879, the mail train departed on time from Edinburgh, carrying passengers bound for the north. By the time it reached the bridge there were between 75 and 90 people on board. The weather was stormy, with gale-force winds and heavy rain. When the train was about halfway across, 13 spans of the bridge collapsed. The train fell into the river below. There were no survivors. This was the Tay Bridge Disaster.

Despite the strong wind, the bridge should have stood. There must have been something else. Today, scientists believe the bridge was struck simultaneously by two tornadoes. It was the tornadoes that destroyed it.

Tornadoes struck Britain again in August 1979, when a tornado outbreak originating in the U.S. midwestern and New England states crossed the Atlantic. They reached the Irish Sea during the Fastnet Race, in which yachts sail from the Isle of Wight, off the south coast of England, to the Fastnet Rock, off southwest Ireland, around the rock and back to Plymouth. In that year, of 306 vessels that entered the race, only 85 completed it. The storms whipped up by the tornadoes were so severe that 23 yachts sank or had to be abandoned and 18 of the sailors died.

Any tornado that crosses a populated area will cause severe damage and injury, but as the years turn into centuries, the details of such events are often lost. We know no more about the tornado that struck Wellesbourne, Warwickshire, England, in 1140 than that it caused extensive damage. A little more is known about the one that struck Nottingham, England, on July 7, 1558. It destroyed every house and church within a mile of the city and trees were thrown more than 200 feet. One child was lifted to a height of 100 feet, then dropped.

European tornadoes are mild compared with American ones. Five or six people were killed by the 1558 Nottingham tornado, but in June 1865 the tornado that moved through Viroqua, Wisconsin, claimed more than 20 lives.

Tornado outbreaks have afflicted Tornado Alley (see page 85) many times. In the 1925 outbreak about seven tornadoes killed a total of 689 people in Missouri, Illinois, and Indiana. There was another major outbreak, affecting 11 states, in May 1973 and, of course, the Super Outbreak of April 1974, which was followed by a second outbreak on the night of June 8. There was another outbreak on April 4, 1977, affecting West Virginia, Virginia, Alabama, Mississippi, Georgia, Tennessee, and Kentucky. It caused 40 deaths and damage costing an estimated $275 million. At least 65 people were hurt and five died in a smaller outbreak that passed through Kalamazoo, Michigan, on May 13, 1980. On April 2 and 3, 1982, an outbreak affected Ohio, Texas, Arkansas, Mississippi, and Missouri, and on May 11 and 12, another outbreak struck Kansas, Oklahoma, and Texas, causing damage estimated to cost $200 million. On March 28, 1984, more than 70 people died in an outbreak in the Carolinas, and from May 6 to 9 an outbreak in Appalachia left 6,000 people homeless when floods added to the tornado damage.

Severe outbreaks continue. Most years see one or two. One of the most serious of recent years occurred from May 18 to 20, 1983, when at least 59 tornadoes moved through Texas, Tennessee, Missouri, Georgia, Louisiana, Mississippi, and Kentucky. In Houston, Texas, 350 homes were destroyed and more than 20 people died. Another, in the Great Plains and midwestern states on June 8, 1984, generated 49 tornadoes. Barneveld, Wisconsin, was totally demolished. A Kansas outbreak, on April 26, 1991, produced more than 70 tornadoes. Up to 45 tornadoes affected 11 states, from Texas to Ohio, in an outbreak from November 21 to 23, 1992.

An outbreak crossed Pennsylvania, Ohio, and New York on May 31, 1985, then crossed into Ontario, Canada. Several Pennsylvania towns were almost totally destroyed and at least 88 people died. Texas, the Carolinas, Virginia, Louisiana, and Oklahoma were affected by an outbreak that also caused severe flooding on May 6, 1989. There was an outbreak in Indiana, Illinois, and Wisconsin on June 2 and 3, 1990, and Alabama, Georgia, the Carolinas, and Tennessee were struck on March 27, 1994, by tornadoes that killed 42 people.

The 1985 tornadoes were not the only ones to afflict Canada. On July 31, 1987, five of them struck a trailer park and a nearby industrial center at Edmonton, Alberta. The tornadoes were relatively mild, with winds of only 60 MPH, but their target was vulnerable and more than 25 people died.

Tornadoes can form in winter as well as summer, provided the storms that trigger them are violent enough. From December 12 to 16, 1987, storms that generated blizzards in Arkansas also produced tornadoes.

Outbreaks last for hours or days, but individual tornadoes seldom last longer than seconds or minutes. That they can wreak such appalling havoc in so short a time is a measure of their ferocity.

In 1973, for example, a fairly weak tornado, with winds of only 100 MPH, struck San Justo, Argentina. It lasted for only three minutes, but in that time it killed 60 people and injured more than 300. At Maravilha, Brazil, about 10 people died in a tornado on October 9, 1984. The tornado that destroyed a Mississippi shopping mall on Friday, January 10, 1975, was also brief, but it had time to kill 12 people and injure a further 200, and a tornado killed at least 10 people in Marion, Illinois, on May 29, 1982, during the few minutes before it died. Several tornadoes struck Water Valley, Mississippi, on April 21, 1984, killing 15 people, and five days later more than half the buildings in Morris, Oklahoma, were demolished by a tornado that killed a total of 14 people in and near the town. Saragosa, Texas, suffered a tornado on May 22, 1987, which killed 29 people and 119 homes were destroyed and 18 people were killed by one in Huntsville, Alabama, on November 15, 1989. Plainfield, Illinois, was struck on August 28, 1990, by a tornado that killed 29 people and injured 300.

Major tropical cyclones are often accompanied by tornadoes. Hurricane Gilbert, which crossed the Caribbean and Gulf of Mexico from September 12 to 17, 1988, generated nearly 40 in Texas alone. In 1989, Hurricane Hugo, which crossed the Caribbean islands and the eastern United States from September 17 to 21, 1989, also triggered tornadoes at Awendaw, South Carolina.

Tornadoes are uncommon in Africa, but on May 20, 1977, Moundou, Chad, was struck by one. Again it was soon over, but not before 13 people had died and 100 had been injured.

Away from the cyclones moving north from the Bay of Bengal, tornadoes are not common in India, either, but the subcontinent is not altogether immune. It took no more than two minutes for 32 people to die and 700 to be injured when a tornado struck northern Delhi on March 17, 1978.

During the spring and fall cyclone seasons however, Bangladesh and the Indian states of West Bengal and Orissa, bordering the Bay of Bengal, are regions almost as dangerous as Tornado Alley. In Bangladesh, a tornado injured more than 200 people and killed 19 when it struck at least 12 villages on April 10, 1976, and on April 1 of the following year an even more destructive one killed more than 600 people and injured about 1,500 in Madaripur and Kishorganj. About 70 people were killed, 1,500 injured, and 15,000 homes destroyed at Noakhali, on April 12, 1981, and 12 died and 200 were hurt at Khulna on April 26, 1983. A tornado at Sripur, on April 10, 1991, destroyed a textile mill, and the country suffered two tornadoes the following month, on May 7 at Tungi and on May 9 at Sirajganj. In five minutes on January 8, 1993, a tornado in the Sylhet and Sunamganj districts killed 32 people and injured more than 1,000.

The worst tornado to strike Bangladesh in recent times struck more than 20 villages on April 26, 1989. It left about 1,000 people dead, 12,000 injured, and nearly 30,000 homeless.

In April 1978, Orissa, India, was struck by a tornado that killed nearly 500 people and wounded more than 1,000, and later the same month about 100 people died in a tornado in West Bengal. Orissa was struck again on April 12, 1981, when a tornado devastated four villages, killing more than 120 people, injuring hundreds, and destroying 2,000 homes. On April 9, 1993, 100 people died when a tornado destroyed five villages in West Bengal.

Most typhoons originating in the South China Sea form in summer and fall. They sometimes bring tornadoes to eastern China, but, like tornadoes everywhere, those in eastern Asia observe no rules. They should not happen as early as April or May, but on April 11, 1983, one killed 54 people in Fujian Province, China, just across the strait from Taiwan, and in May several tornadoes in central Vietnam killed nearly 80 people.

Farther north, off the East China Sea, 14 towns were seriously damaged and at least 16 people were killed and more than 400 injured when a tornado struck Heilongjiang Province, China, on July 31, 1987.

Throughout the world and throughout history, tornadoes have appeared, with little or no warning, and wrought havoc in communities they have crossed. There are more in some years than in others, but there is no evident pattern to their changing frequency. It is possible, however, that tornadoes could become more frequent in the future. Many scientists believe that, by releasing into the atmosphere carbon dioxide and a range of other gases that absorb heat, we may cause an enhanced "greenhouse effect." This would make climates generally grow warmer and might lead to more large-scale thunderstorms, some of which would be tornadic.

Measuring the severity of tornadoes

Any tornado that crosses a populated area will cause damage, but not every tornado causes the same amount of damage. Tornadoes vary quite widely in strength. Some generate winds of only 60 MPH or even less, others of 300 MPH or more, and in the great majority of cases the wind speed lies somewhere between these extremes.

Obviously it would be very useful if scientists could arrange tornadoes in categories according to their force. This would allow them to see whether, on average, tornadoes are stronger in certain regions than in others. The resulting information would provide guidance for builders and emergency services by telling them the worst conditions structures and communities are likely to encounter. When a tornado warning is issued, it might also make it possible to include a forecast of the force people should expect. Finally, a comprehensive categorization of tornadoes as they occur would provide meteorologists with valuable data to help in their studies of tornadic storms.

Unfortunately, the scientific study of tornadoes is extremely difficult (see page 107). The vortices appear very briefly and without warning, so there is a large element of luck in whether a team of tornado-hunters is present when one occurs.

Even if scientists are in the right place at the right time, their problems are not solved. They must find some way to measure conditions at the center of the tornado vortex and immediately around it. The conventional instrument for measuring wind speed is called an *anemometer*. There are several designs, but the commonest consists of small cups mounted at the end of horizontal arms attached so they can turn freely about a vertical axis. When the wind blows, the arms spin, and their rate of spin is converted into wind speed. Alternatively, the anemometer may measure the pressure exerted by the wind, with a vane to keep the instrument facing into the wind. Anemometers work well with most of the winds we experience, but the winds inside a tornado would demolish them instantly and scatter their remains over a vast area.

There is another way to approach the problem. It still requires direct measurement, but at least the instruments can be made more robust.

Wind is the movement of air from a region of relatively high atmospheric pressure to one where the pressure is lower. The wind does not flow in a straight line, directly from high to low, but spirals inward (see page 13) near the surface and at higher levels flows around the center of low pressure. The speed of the wind is determined by the *pressure gradient*, which is difference in atmospheric pressure between the high- and low-pressure centers. The greater the pressure gradient, the stronger the wind, and the relationship between the two is determined by well-known physical laws. If you know one, the other can be calculated. To calculate the wind speed inside a tornado, therefore, all you need do is measure the atmospheric pressure some distance away from the tornado and the pressure at its center. It is still necessary to place a barometer

Figure 29: *TOTO (Totable Tornado Observatory) being tested in a wind tunnel in 1983.* (Copyright: Howard B. Bluestein).

inside the tornado, but at least barometers have no moving parts exposed to the wind.

This method would work in principle, but the original difficulties are not really resolved. Scientists still have to find the tornadoes they wish to examine and then install their instruments without being killed or injured, and the instruments themselves must survive to be recovered later. A barometer can be made much stronger than an anemometer, but it is doubtful whether any instrument could withstand a wind of more than 200 MPH.

Nevertheless, it has been attempted. TOTO, developed by Alfred J. Bedard and Carl Ramzy at the NOAA (National Oceanic and Atmospheric Administration) Environmental Research Laboratory in Boulder, Colorado, is a robust cylinder in a casing of half-inch aluminum set in a frame of angle iron, with arms holding instruments to measure wind speed, pressure, temperature, and electrical discharges. It carries its own batteries and records the data it obtains. The initials of its name stand for Totable Tornado Observatory and also spell the name of Dorothy's dog in *The Wonderful Wizard of Oz*. TOTO weighs 400 pounds and has made many measurements of mesocyclones, but it is designed only for winds up to 200 MPH. Winds stronger than this would probably topple it.

Suppose, though, that scientists were able to infer the conditions inside a tornado from the effects it caused. The force needed to uproot a mature tree, for example, or demolish a building can be calculated accurately, so it might be possible to work out the force of a tornado by the damage it caused. This is the approach adopted by Tetsuya Theodore Fujita. Professor of meteorology at the University of Chicago, he has spent half a century studying tornadoes.

Fujita began by making detailed examinations of the trails left by some 250 tornadoes and tornado outbreaks. With his colleague Allen Pearson, formerly the chief tornado forecaster for the National Weather Service, in 1971 he devised what is now known as the Fujita Tornado Intensity Scale. It is a six-point scale that relates wind speed to the extent of the damage the wind is likely to cause and it is often used to describe tornadoes.

In the United States, 69% of all tornadoes are weak, 29% are strong, and only 2% are violent. An F-0 tornado causes very little damage. Branches may be broken from trees and loose tiles ripped from roofs. At F-1, windows may be broken and some trees blown down. F-2 indicates a much more serious event. Mature trees may be uprooted and flimsy structures, such as mobile homes, demolished. With winds approaching 200 MPH, an F-3 tornado will overturn cars, demolish walls, and flatten trees. Beyond these categories, tornadoes are described as violent. An F-4 tornado can demolish a house, leaving it a pile of rubble, and one rated F-5 has the power to demolish houses and scatter the debris over a wide area. Even steel-framed buildings will be severely damaged and cars may be picked up and carried several hundred feet.

The Fujita scale is not based on measurements of wind speed, but on assessments of the effects of tornadoes and calculations of the force needed to produce those effects. Nowadays, however, meteorologists often observe tornadoes with Doppler radar, which allows direct measurement of wind speed from a distance.

FUJITA TORNADO INTENSITY SCALE

Rating	Wind speed (mph)	Damaged expected
Weak		
F-0	40–72	Light damage
F-1	73–112	Moderate damage
Strong		
F-2	113–157	Considerable damage
F-3	157–206	Severe damage
Violent		
F-4	207–260	Devastating damage
F-5	261–318	Incredible damage

Radar exploits the fact that all forms of electromagnetic radiation travel at the speed of light and that at certain wavelengths (the distance between one wave crest and the next) radiation is reflected by objects it strikes. Water droplets strongly reflect radiation with a wavelength of about 10 cm, so this is the wavelength used for weather radar. It can reveal the structure of clouds by showing where their water is concentrated and the level at which rising water freezes and falling ice melts. By measuring the time that elapses between a radiation pulse leaving the transmitter and the receipt of its reflection, it is possible to calculate the distance between the radar transmitter and the reflective water droplets.

Doppler radar is based on the fact that the wavelength of radiation emitted by a source will decrease if the source is moving toward an observer and increase if it is moving away. Discovered in 1842 by the Austrian physicist Christian Doppler (see volume 6 for more details), this is called the *Doppler effect*. It applies to radiation of any kind (Doppler proposed it for the case of light, but it was first tested with sound) and to reflected radiation as well as radiation from a primary source.

Transmit a pulse of radiation, the wavelength of which is known very precisely, measure equally precisely the wavelength of its reflection, and comparing the two reveals whether the source of the reflection is moving toward or away from the observer and at what speed. If the object reflecting the pulse is approaching, the wavelength received will be shorter than the wavelength transmitted. It is said to be *blue-shifted*, because when this happens to visible light the change is toward the shorter-wave, blue end of the light spectrum. If the object is receding, the wavelength received will be longer than that transmitted, or *red-shifted*, toward the longwave, red end of the spectrum. The amount by which the radiation has been blue- or red-shifted indicates the speed with which the object is approaching or receding.

Scan an object in this way and if the Doppler radar indicates that one side is approaching and the other side retreating, clearly the object must be rotating, and the amount of wavelength shift reveals its speed of rotation. This is how Doppler radar is used to tell whether there is a rotational motion of water droplets inside a cloud. If there is, and it is big and fast enough, the cloud contains a mesocyclone.

Doppler radar is now used to study weather systems from a distance of 100 miles or more, but there are a few disadvantages. Not every cloud with rotating currents develops into a mesocyclone and generates tornadoes, for example, so results need careful interpretation. Also, the curvature of the Earth prevents radars from detecting distant air movements close to the ground because they are beyond the horizon, and therefore hidden from radiation that travels in a straight line, and the radars may have difficulty with line-squall storms moving across the field of view, from left to right or right to left. This is because the Doppler effect refers only to objects moving toward or away from the observer. This problem is resolved by using two Doppler radars, observing from different positions to give a more three-dimensional view.

As the technology continues to improve, meteorologists will have an increasing number of tools at their disposal. In years to come these will allow them to make much more detailed observations of conditions inside tornadic storms and to measure the severity of tornadoes much more precisely.

Studying tornadoes

Tornado hunters have a hard time. Working on the ground, they must drive to likely areas then cruise around, constantly searching the sky for storm clouds that look promising. It is a somewhat hit-or-miss operation, and if they are lucky enough to spot a tornado they have only a few minutes in which to unload the instruments

Radiosondes and rawinsondes

Weather stations throughout the world use balloons to study atmospheric conditions above ground level and to a height of about 80,000 feet, in the middle of the stratosphere. Balloons were first used for this purpose in 1927. Modern versions are called *radiosondes*, because they take "soundings" (measurements) and transmit them to receiving stations by radio. To make sure that measurements from around the world can be combined to produce a comprehensive picture of atmospheric conditions at a particular time, every weather station, no matter where it is, releases one radiosonde every day at midnight and a second at noon Greenwich Mean Time. The National Meteorological Center, in Washington, D.C., receives about 2,500 sets of radiosonde data every day.

The balloon itself is spherical, about five feet in diameter, and filled with hydrogen. Beneath it is a cable 30 meters (nearly 100 feet) long with a package of instruments attached to its lower end. The cable needs to be this long to make sure air movements around the balloon do not interfere with instrument readings. The standard instrument package comprises a very sensitive thermometer, a hygrometer to measure humidity, and a barometer to measure air pressure. There are also timers, switches to turn the instruments on and off at predetermined times, a radio transmitter, batteries to supply power, and a parachute to return the instruments safely to the ground.

After it is released, the radiosonde climbs steadily, at about 15 feet per second. As it rises, its hydrogen expands, and when it reaches a height of around 80,000 feet the balloon bursts and its instruments parachute to the ground, from where they are recovered and returned to the weather station from which they were launched. During its flight, the radiosonde broadcasts its measurements to the ground station.

In addition to its instruments, the radiosonde carries a radar reflector immediately below the balloon. This strongly reflects radar pulses and allows the movement of the radiosonde to be tracked from the ground. Before radar was invented, balloons were tracked visually, but, of course, they disappeared from view as soon as they entered cloud.

As it ascends, the radiosonde moves horizontally with the wind, which usually changes direction and speed in different layers of air. Tracking the radiosonde provides accurate information on the wind speed and direction in each atmospheric level through which the device passes. Balloons that are tracked to study winds at very great heights are sometimes called *rawinsondes* (for radar wind-sounding). In years to come these will probably broadcast their precise locations using the Global Positioning System.

from their van, install them in the path of the approaching storm, and get out of the way before it arrives.

They have clues, of course. Before setting out they will have analyzed information from the National Weather Service. What interests them is not so much the ordinary weather forecast, but the data returned from meteorological balloons, called *radiosondes* or, if they are used primarily to study high-altitude winds, *rawinsondes* (see box). Meteorologists first began using radiosondes in 1927 and nowadays they are released from weather stations all over the world. In order to ensure that the data they provide can be built into a comprehensive picture of the weather at a particular time, every participating weather station, no matter where it is in the world, releases two radiosondes each day, one at midnight and one at noon Greenwich Mean Time.

The tornado hunters based at the National Severe Storms Laboratory in Norman, Oklahoma, tune into the early-morning broadcast of radiosonde data. These start arriving at the National Meteorological Center in Washington, D.C., soon after 7 P.M., which is midnight at Greenwich. The hunters look for places where the air temperature drops very sharply with increasing height and where the wind increases in speed and changes direction rapidly. Supported by data about the movement of weather systems, this indicates a collision between three air masses, with potentially unstable air trapped beneath a stable layer, and strong wind shear aloft. These are ideal conditions for the formation of severe thunderstorms that may link into squall lines.

As they drive, the team of hunters keep in contact with the changing meteorological situation by radio, mobile telephones, and a miniature TV. The information they received before setting out guides them to the general area in which tornadic storms may be expected. Constant updates include the results of Doppler radar scans of cloud patterns (see page 100). These will identify cumulonimbus clouds and the location of thunderstorms that have developed mesocyclones and supercells.

Even at this stage, finding a tornado is a matter of chance and when one is found it may start to chase the hunters, forcing them to flee before they have time to set up their instruments. Even with the help of radiosonde data and constantly updated weather reports, most hunters can expect to see no more than one or two tornadoes a year and none in some years, for which they will drive thousands of miles. Professor T. Theodore Fujita, a world authority on tornadoes who has spent half a century studying them, has never had a really good, close look at one. Unless you go looking for them, you may never see a tornado in your entire life.

You should hope never to see a tornado and on no account must you ever go out in pursuit of them. Professional tornado hunters are highly trained. They can judge the way a tornado is moving and know when and how to keep out of its way. Lacking their experience, you might be caught, and even the mildest tornadoes are extremely dangerous.

While they search, the scientists record a running commentary, describing their location and the weather conditions they can see. Once they locate a tornado, they prepare to make their observations and measurements. The team carries a video camera to provide a visual record and for some years used the TOTO (Totable Tornado Observatory) to measure temperature, wind speed, and pressure inside the vortex (see page 99). Today there is an improved version of TOTO, called Turtle, that may prove more robust, and portable

Figure 30: *University of Oklahoma graduate students probing a tornado in north-central Oklahoma with a portable Doppler radar on April 12, 1991.* (Copyright: Howard B. Bluestein)

Doppler radar (see page 100) is also available to them. At one time, some scientists believed winds inside the most powerful tornadoes might flow faster than the speed of sound (in air at 68° F this is about 770 MPH). Portable Doppler radar instruments have measured wind speeds close to 300 MPH and scientists now believe this is as fast as they ever blow.

A radar signal travels like a beam of light and it has the same limitation as a flashlight beam. A flashlight is very good at illuminating nearby objects, but those farther away are not nearly so well lit. This is because the beam diverges. The farther it travels the wider it becomes, so its light is spread over an area that increases with distance. The amount of light does not change, so as the area covered increases, the amount of light received at each small part of it must decrease. The size of objects it will reveal clearly is called the *resolution* of the flashlight or radar.

Resolution is especially important for Doppler radar because it relies on accurate measurements of the wavelength of signals reflected from different parts of the object being examined. In the early years of their use, portable Doppler radars were unable to resolve details as small as an average tornado from a distance of a few miles, which is often as close as tornado hunters can get. Increasing the size of the transmitting and receiving antennas would improve resolution, but it would also make the apparatus much more cumbersome and prone to damage in the strong winds along the gust front of a squall line. Instead, a group of engineers at the University of Massachusetts at Amherst made a set of radar equipment that works at a much shorter wavelength, allowing it to transmit a much narrower beam. The narrow beam provides the needed improvement in resolution without increasing the size of the antennas, but at a price. The equipment costs more and uses more power, and under some weather conditions the reflections it receives can be difficult to interpret.

No pilot would willingly fly through a tornado, but tornadic storms are studied from the air, using specially equipped and strengthened airplanes. Planes fly over, around, and through cumulonimbus clouds on carefully planned routes, recording vertical air currents, winds, temperatures, pressures, electrical activity, and a range of other characteristics. The information they gather helps scientists understand how thunderstorms develop and what goes on inside huge storm clouds.

Rawinsondes are also used, and they can be launched directly into storms and their movements tracked. In 1986, this technique resulted in the first direct measurements obtained from inside a tornadic storm. These showed that the upcurrents were rising at more than 100 MPH.

Other scientists have an entirely different way of studying the way events occur naturally. They can use computers to construct models. The first computer models were made in the 1960s, but it was not until the 1980s, with the invention of supercomputers, that scientists had access to sufficient computing power and speed to begin modeling weather systems.

Computer models are entirely mathematical. Those of weather phenomena begin with the equations describing known physical behavior. They make it possible to calculate, for example, what happens when air is warmed from below, how it cools as it rises and expands, what happens as its water vapor condenses or evaporates, how air masses at different temperatures and densities react when they meet, and how pressure gradients, vorticity, and the Coriolis effect influence wind speed and direction.

For modeling purposes, the atmosphere is divided into "blocks" by means of a three-dimensional grid of vertical and horizontal lines, all of which meet at right angles. All the equations are used to make calculations at every point where grid lines intersect. The finer the grid, the more accurate the model will be, but the finer the grid the more intersections it will have and, therefore, the more calculations that must be made. Computer modelers strive constantly to improve their accuracy by working with ever finer grids.

Once the basic equations have been programmed and the grid constructed, data must be fed into the computer so numbers can be substituted for the symbols in the equations. The numbers must be genuine, obtained by making measurements of the actual conditions at a particular place and time. This is where the measurements made by tornado hunters go. They are passed on to the modelers and fed into computers.

When this task is completed, the model can be set running. At each grid intersection, the condition of the air will be calculated and the results passed to neighboring intersections as data that alters conditions there. Alterations mean the relevant values must be recalculated, producing changed conditions that pass as data to more intersections. Step by step, the entire system changes its characteristics as the computer calculates and recalculates the changes taking place at every grid intersection. Millions of calculations are needed to show changes that would take only a few minutes in a real weather system, so if the model is to produce useful results in a reasonable time it must work very fast indeed. That is why such models can be made only with the fastest, most powerful supercomputers in the world.

When the computer run ends, the result will be a system in a different state from that in which it commenced. In a sense, the model will have predicted that if the weather, or developing storm, starts in the way the input data described, after so many minutes or hours this is what will have happened to it. Perhaps it will have dissipated, leaving a clear sky. Or maybe it will have grown into a huge and violent storm. Or, if conditions are right, perhaps it will have formed a supercell and caused one or more tornadoes.

This is all very well, but before scientists can trust the result of all these millions of calculations they must check to see what happened out in the real world. This is what scientists call "ground truth," observing what really happens outside, "on the ground." This is another job for the tornado hunters, although in their case it is a job they have already done. As well as recording conditions in and around a tornadic storm, they will also have monitored its progress. They will know what really happened to it and this can be compared with what the computer "predicted" should have happened. If the two agree, and if they continue to agree often many tests of this kind, the model will be accepted as reliable.

Then it can be used to simulate the real world by performing experiments. Scientists can ask it direct questions. Is this what starts an upcurrent rotating? How fast must that rotation be before it extends downward in a tornado funnel? What happens as the upcurrents and downcurrents separate and the storm becomes a supercell?

Supercells can now be accurately modeled in this way, and as finer and finer grids are used the models reveal increasing amounts of detail. Very lifelike tornado vortices have been produced inside computers. Because the modelers had to feed in the data to produce those "virtual" vortices, this means they are very close to understanding the way they occur. A scientific picture of the birth, life, and death of a tornadic storm is being painted, detail by ever finer detail.

It does not mean tornado hunters can pack up their vans and go home. Ground truth will always be needed, partly to keep a check on the models as they continue to advance. Left to themselves, the models could easily diverge from reality until they came to generate simulations that were very convincing, but quite wrong and, therefore, harmful, because they would seriously mislead forecasters. Observers will also be needed to supply more and more data. Tornadoes refuse to be bound by rules and a complete understanding of one, "average" tornado does not necessarily mean the mechanisms of all tornadoes have been mastered.

In the coming years, modelers and tornado hunters will continue to collaborate. The practical result of their efforts will be improved tornado forecasts.

Tracking and forecasting tornadoes

Tornadoes are unpredictable, almost by definition. Despite this, their progress can be tracked once they have appeared and people can be warned whenever there is a likehood of them. Not so many years ago, and well within the memory of people who are still alive, the first sign of an approaching tornado was often the distinctive roar it made or its actual appearance. Everyone who could would run for shelter and hope they reached it in time. There was no time to do much that might have made their homes more secure. Tornadoes are still far from being tamed, or even fully understood, but meteorology has advanced greatly in modern times. Today there is usually, although not always, time to prepare for the onslaught. At present, the National Weather Service can provide about six minutes' warning between the time a tornado touches the ground and its arrival in a populated area. This safety margin is likely to improve considerably in the next few years.

Weather systems move and each one affects an area of hundreds of square miles. There is no possibility of plotting its movement or forecasting how it will behave unless the system can be seen as a whole, all of it displayed at once on a map. No matter how many people record measurements of temperature, wind, pressure, and rainfall in different places, until their observations have been collected, no overall picture can emerge.

Scientists realized two centuries ago the need to collect information from scattered locations, but in those days the fastest travel was by galloping horse and the task was impossible. They did what they could, even so, collecting measurements all made at about the same time and compiling them to produce *synoptic charts*, much like the weather maps you see today in newspapers and on TV. A synoptic chart is one recording the situation at a particular time (the word is from the Greek *sunoptikos*, meaning "seen all together"). Charts of this kind were being compiled in France by the late 18th century, but by the time they could be drawn the situation they recorded was 10 years old. Scientific weather forecasting was out of the question.

What the meteorologists needed was some means of communicating the results of measurements as fast as they were obtained, and the breakthrough for which they had been waiting so long came in 1844. That was the year in which the first telegraph line in the world was constructed. It ran only between Baltimore and Washington, D.C., but was so successful that similar lines were soon linking towns in many countries.

Samuel Morse, who claimed to have invented the telegraph, devised the code used to transmit messages along it (see volume 6 for more details). The code, bearing his name, is little used today, but it was simple, easy to learn, and transmitting it required very little electrical power. It was based on combinations of only two signals, one short (called a "dot" and conventionally written as .), the other long (called a "dash" and conventionally written as -). In Morse code, for example, the word "tornado" is: _ ___ ._. _. ._ ___. It looks cumbersome, but a skilled operator could send it very fast. Because it used only two signals it is known as a "binary" code, and it demonstrated the versatility of binary codes generally. In modern times this led to the use of another binary code, written using 0 and 1 to symbolize the "on" and "off" positions of a switch, as the basis for all computer programming.

Meteorologists could now communicate and weather stations were established all over America and Europe. Eventually these formed a network covering the whole world, although still rather unevenly. There are now about 2,500 surface weather stations throughout the world and in addition some 1,500 ships also report meteorological observations. To ensure that the observations can be combined to produce a description of the weather at the same time everywhere, stations try to report readings taken at midnight, 0600, noon, and 1800 hours Greenwich Mean Time (Z) every day. The data they obtain are coordinated and analyzed by a system called World Weather Watch, organized by the World Meteorological Organization, which is a United Nations agency.

For a long time observations were made only from the ground. Then, when lightweight but robust instruments became available in the 1920s, balloons came into use for measuring conditions above the surface and eventually in the upper atmosphere (see page 102). Today there are about 500 weather stations reporting upper-air measurements. Between their two ascents to collect full data, at 0600 and 1800 Z wind balloons carrying only radar reflectors are launched and tracked simply to monitor wind direction and strength.

Aircraft are also used. Some civil airliners carry instruments to monitor atmospheric conditions. Such aircraft reports are irregular, however, because their timing and location are controlled by flight schedules and routes, and this reduces their scientific value. Airplanes are much more useful for direct observation than for routine monitoring. By the late 1940s there were planes strong enough to fly into thunderstorms, and today specially strengthened aircraft, equipped with sensitive instruments, fly regularly through cumulonimbus clouds and around the central cores of storms, different types of plane working at each altitude up to 30,000 feet and beyond.

Even then, an overall picture had to be compiled from many local observations. Each weather station, balloon, ship, or aircraft can report only the conditions at a particular place. It was impossible to see and measure a weather system the size of a continent or ocean all at once, but the next major step brought that wide view much closer.

On April 1, 1960, the Television and Infrared Observation Satellite (TIROS) was launched into Earth orbit. It circled the Earth, transmitting to ground stations television pictures of the narrow strips of land and sea over which it was passing. TIROS observed only part of the Earth, missing the polar regions, and its pictures were somewhat fuzzy, but it revealed new possibilities. In particular, it provided much more detail than had been obtainable earlier. Surface weather stations are many miles apart and upper-air observation stations are even more widely dispersed, so what was happening between them, in the gaps where no observations could be made, had to be filled in by informed guessing. Satellite pictures resolve details only a mile or two across and there are no gaps. They show patterns of cloud, great swirls around depressions, individual cumulus-causing showers, and entire frontal systems.

Dozens of meteorological satellites now orbit the Earth. TIROS has descendants, two satellites both called TIROS-N, and these have been joined by two Geostationary Operational Environmental Satellites (GOES). The latest of these, GOES-8, carrying more advanced cameras and instruments than its predecessors, was launched on April 13, 1994. TIROS and GOES are United States satellites operated by the National Oceanic and Atmospheric Administration (NOAA). The European Union monitors the weather over Europe with three Meteosats, Russia operates the Elektro satellite over the Indian Ocean, and there are also Chinese and Japanese weather satellites. Together, satellites now monitor the entire planet. There are no longer any gaps, at least from space.

Weather satellites are placed in either a *sun-synchronous*, or *polar*, orbit or in a *geosynchronous*, or *geostationary*, or *Clarke*, orbit (after the author Arthur C. Clarke, who first thought of it). A sun-synchronous orbit is at a height equal to one-seventh the radius of the Earth, about 534 miles, and at a slight angle to the lines of longitude so the orbit is fixed in relation to the position of the Sun. The satellite takes 102 minutes to circle the Earth, passing close to both poles (but not exactly over them). As the satellite orbits, the Earth is turning beneath it, so each swath it covers, 1,700 miles wide, lies beside the one over which it passed in its previous orbit. In the course of 12 hours it passes over every point on the Earth. Surface stations can tune into transmissions from the satellite as it passes overhead to obtain current information about conditions in their area.

A geosynchronous orbit is at a height equal to 5.6 times the radius of the Earth, about 22,370 miles above the equator. The satellite moves in the same direction as the Earth rotates and at the same speed (at that height, 6,850 MPH), so it remains permanently above the same point on the surface. It has a view of very nearly an entire hemisphere, although its resolution at the edges is poorer than that closer to its position. WWW maintains five satellites in geosynchronous orbits spaced evenly around the equator to provide a good view of the entire world. Instruments on a satellite in geosynchronous orbit scan its field of view slowly, taking 20 minutes to complete a scan. The resolution is almost as good as that from satellites in much lower sun-synchronous orbits, and pictures can be taken at night using infrared cameras.

The latest recruit to the observational network over the United States is a nationwide Doppler radar cover called NEXRAD (Next Generation Weather Radar). The first installations came into operation in the early 1990s, and by 1996 the completed system comprised 175 of them, located at weather stations, airports, and military bases. Each looks like a large golf ball mounted on top of tall tower made from scaffolding and it can provide three-dimensional images with clear resolution of weather up to 125 miles away and rather poorer resolution of weather at distances up to 200 miles. These installations are fixed, of course, and much more powerful than the portable Doppler radars used by tornado hunters (see page 100).

Already, Doppler radar has improved the reliability of tornado prediction. Previously, radar was used to study storm clouds. The radar reflection indicated the location of raindrops, and because the more raindrops there are the stronger the reflection will be, it also showed their concentration. Sometimes, a characteristic hook shape can be seen in the rain pattern, to one side of the cloud. In the 1950s, meteorologists came to recognize this as a sign of a mesocyclone, possibly heralding tornadoes. Today they rely on Doppler radar, which measures directly the speed at which air is rotating inside a cloud and is a much more reliable indicator.

All of the information from surface stations, upper-air soundings, ships, aircraft, satellites, and the NEXRAD network is processed to produce the forecasts issued by the National Weather Service. It is a formidable task and one that must be performed quickly if the forecast is to be of any use. In 1980, the Forecast Systems Laboratory at the NOAA Environmental Research Laboratories in Boulder, Colorado, launched the Program for Regional Observing and Forecasting Services (PROFS). Its aim is to find increasingly efficient ways of assimilating incoming information and displaying the result at interactive workstations, then to transfer the technologies to wherever forecasters need them. This is especially important for improving the quality of forecasts issued for the weather up to two hours ahead, called *nowcasting*. These are the forecasts that can give warning of approaching tornadoes.

The skies are being constantly watched by meteorologists studying pictures transmitted from orbiting satellites. These pictures show where large thunderstorms are developing. Wind measurements for the area around the thunderstorm will reveal the presence of high-level wind shear, and surface reports of changing temperature and pressure will allow the scientists to locate air masses and the fronts where different air masses meet. The situation changes as air masses move vertically as well as horizontally, and their development is reported to the ground stations more or less as it occurs, in real time. Large, isolated thunderstorms and squall lines are also watched carefully.

Meteorologists of the National Weather Service are quick to recognize vigorous squall lines and large, isolated cumulonimbus clouds. Incoming reports tell them if these are producing severe weather conditions. If they think it necessary, the forecasters will issue a warning to communities in the path of the advancing storms. These may take the form of a *severe thunderstorm watch*, if thunderstorms are approaching you, followed some time later by a *severe thunderstorms warning*, when they have reached your area. Really big thunderstorms can be dangerous in their own right.

Lightning kills up to 100 people a year in the United States. Hail does not always fall as pellets not much bigger than rice grains. Hailstones can reach the size of softballs and fall with enough force to do serious damage. Wind gusts ahead of an advancing storm may not twist like the wind in a tornado, but they can briefly reach hurricane force. Storm winds of 140 MPH have been measured, which is sufficient to strip away a roof or demolish a mobile home. Finally, storms bring torrential rain and this can lead to flash floods, which kill more people than any other weather phenomenon.

Most national weather services issue warnings of severe weather, but it is only in the United States that meteorologists are especially alert to the risk of tornadoes. They pore over satellite photographs, looking for the telltale "hook" in the cloud formation that indicates the presence of a mesocyclone and analyze Doppler radar images that tell them if the interior of a cloud is spinning, and how fast.

The first warning they broadcast is a *tornado watch*. It means tornadoes have not yet been observed, but the conditions are right for them and they may develop in the next few hours.

You should always take this warning seriously. When you hear the message the sky may be blue, the Sun shining, and the air calm. Remember, though, that the forecasters are tracking a storm or squall line that may be moving fast, but is still a long way from you. Do not be deceived by the fine weather. If you hear on the radio that storms are coming, believe what you hear. Even if the forecasters are wrong, which is unlikely, it is best to heed their warnings.

The second warning is a *tornado warning*. It means a tornado has been reported in your area. If you hear this, you must find shelter immediately. You could be lucky, of course, and the tornado might never reach you, but it is foolish to take risks and even if no tornado arrives, the rain, hail, and lightning almost certainly will.

Damage from tornadoes

Forecasters can warn of an approaching tornado, but they can only guess at its severity. The Fujita Tornado Intensity Scale (see page 100) ranks tornadoes by their wind speed and the damage they cause, but only after the event. Scientists assess the damage the tornado caused and use this to work out its force. Obviously, they can do this only after the tornado has disappeared. Until it arrives, therefore, no one can tell whether it will merely break a few branches from trees and damage some chimneys or flatten well-built houses and throw cars around like toys.

A strong (F-2 and F-3) or violent (F-4 and F-5) tornado is likely to produce freak effects. A house was once transported two miles and another was lifted, turned through 90 degrees, and gently set down again on the same spot. A roof was once blown 12 miles. A woman living at El Dorado, Texas, is said to have survived being blown through a window of her house and carried 60 feet by a tornado on June 10, 1958.

More commonly, though, tornadoes simply destroy property, and although improved forecasting and advice about how to survive have reduced the number of fatalities, the number of injuries and amount of property damage remain high. In the United States, property damage has tended to increase over the years. Damage is measured as monetary cost, so this is due partly to the rise in property values. It is also due to the growth in popularity of vacation homes, built to lower standards than would be demanded in cities, and mobile homes. Outside the United States, in countries where warning systems are less advanced and large numbers of people live in poorly constructed housing in sprawling urban areas, the risk of death and injury is much higher.

Flying debris causes as much property damage as direct exposure to the wind and is probably responsible for most tornado injuries. The funnel itself is narrow, but winds around the core demolish

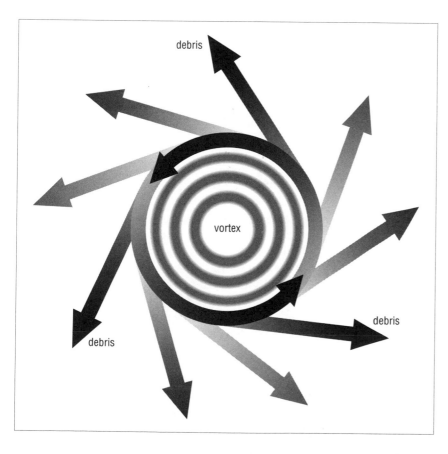

Figure 31: *How debris sprays out from a tornado.*

anything in their path. This produces solid fragments of all sizes that at first whirl around the vortex in upcurrents strong enough to keep them airborne. They move in a circular path because the centripetal force, acting toward the center of the vortex, balances the momentum directing them in a straight line. That balance is unstable, and after a few moments the momentum of the fragments exceeds the centripetal force. When that happens fragments spray out from the funnel, each item flying in a straight line at a tangent to the vortex (see figure 31). As it advances, the tornado hurls debris outward in all directions, like a spinning gun, but one with the capacity to reload constantly as it gathers fresh debris to spin and throw.

A moving object possesses energy due to its motion. This is called *kinetic energy*. If it collides with another object it loses part or all of its kinetic energy. This energy does not simply vanish. It may be transferred to the other object, setting it in motion. This is what happens on a pool table when one ball strikes another and makes it roll. Eventually, all the kinetic energy dissipates, converted into heat, but it is the transfer of kinetic energy that causes damage. How much damage depends on the amount of kinetic energy the moving object possessed. This is proportional to the mass of the object and the square of its velocity (see box on page 115), which means that speed is much more important than mass. If, for example, a mass of one pound moves at 45 feet per second, its kinetic energy will be about 32 pounds. Double the mass, to two pounds, and the kinetic energy is 63 pounds. Keep the mass at one pound and double the velocity, to 90 feet per second, and the kinetic energy is 126 pounds.

It requires less energy to accelerate a small mass to high speed than it does to accelerate a large mass, so the speed of fragments ejected from a tornado funnel depends on their size (strictly, their mass, but for most ordinary materials it amounts to roughly the same thing). Obviously, if you are struck by an object the size and weight of a car, you will be injured, even if it is traveling quite slowly, but even the fiercest tornadoes throw out few cars. Contrary to what common sense might suggests, the small items, traveling very fast, are much more dangerous than the large ones. They are also much harder to see.

Walking on a windy day can be difficult. You can feel the wind pushing you this way and that. Air is a physical substance. It has weight (or mass). One cubic foot of air weighs about 0.07 pound. When air moves it also has kinetic energy and the amount is calculated in just the same way as for any other substance. The faster it moves, the more kinetic energy it has, and so the harder it pushes you. In a 30-MPH wind, which is strong enough to push you around when you are out walking, its kinetic energy is about two pounds per cubic foot. If you are, say, 5.5 feet tall and 1 foot wide (width, not waist measurement!) a 30-MPH headwind will push against you

Kinetic energy and wind force

Kinetic energy (KE), the energy of motion, is equal to half of the mass (m) of a moving body multiplied by the square of its velocity (*v*) (or speed). Expressed algebraically, KE = ½mv^2.

This formula gives a result in joules if *m* is in kilograms and *v* is in meters per second. If you need to calculate the force in pounds exerted by a mass measured in pounds moving in miles per hour, the formula must be modified slightly to: KE = $mv^2 \div 2g$, where *v* is converted to feet per second (feet per second = MPH x 5280 ÷ 3600) and *g* is 32 (the acceleration due to gravity in feet per second).

with a force of about 12 pounds. At the wind speeds common around the core of a tornado, the force can be huge. Near the core of a severe tornado (F-3) the wind may be 200 MPH, with a kinetic energy of about 94 pounds per cubic foot. Try walking in that and the wind will press against you with a force of nearly 520 pounds, which is probably about four times the weight of your body.

When a 200-MPH wind slams into the side of a trailer, it hits it with a force of around 10 tons. That smashes the side, opening up gaps for the wind to widen further, but the trailer is not hit from just one direction. Tornadic winds spiral, so as the tornado moves the wind constantly changes direction. Not surprisingly, the trailer disintegrates almost instantly.

Air pressure at the center of a tornado vortex is very low. It used to be believed that if a tornado passed directly over a building, the sudden difference between pressure inside and outside could make the building explode and the way to prevent this was to open the windows before the tornado arrived, to allow air to flow out of the building and equalize the pressure. Indeed, buildings do sometimes appear to explode, but it is the wind and flying debris that cause most of the damage. Once the structure has been breached and seriously weakened, wind blowing through it can make parts of it collapse outward. By that time, of course, the interior and exterior air pressures have equalized. Opening the windows actually increases the likelihood of severe damage, because it provides immediate access to the wind.

Roofs are especially prone to damage in any strong wind. There are several reasons for their vulnerability. Many homes have roofs covered with slates, tiles, or shingles. These are laid in an overlapping pattern and fastened at their upper edges. They cannot be fastened very tightly, because if one breaks it must be possible to remove and replace it without disturbing those around it. Wind can penetrate along the lower edge, exerting an upward force that may be strong enough to dislodge any loose tiles, and once a few have been removed the wind can quickly strip away more.

Some roofs are covered by single sheets of material, but often these are not fixed very securely to the frame of the building. Nails driven at right angles through the sheets and into the roof timbers will hold under most conditions, but if a wind of tornadic force finds a gap under the eaves and pushes upward, they are not too difficult to withdraw.

Most roofs, especially on private homes, slope up to a central ridge. This shape is excellent for allowing rain to flow away quickly and for preventing snow accumulating in a layer thick enough for its weight to damage the structure. In really strong winds, however, ridged roofs do experience a force due to pressure differences above and below. The reason for the reduced pressure above the roof is the same as that which produces the very low air pressure at the center of a tornado vortex.

Figure 32: *During a tornado following Hurricane Andrew, one resident of La Place, Louisiana, was killed when the roof and outside wall of his home collapsed into his bedroom.* (National Hurricane Center, NOAA)

It is called the Bernoulli effect and it was discovered in 1738 by a Swiss mathematician called Daniel Bernoulli (see box on page 117, and volume 6, for more details). If you picture the wind as a mass of air flowing through an imaginary tube, a ridged roof constricts the tube. Air must flow up the roof, over the ridge, and down the other side. This accelerates the wind, because air crossing the roof must travel farther than air to either side of the roof, but it must do so in the same length of time. In cross section, the roof forms a triangle and the air has to travel along two of its sides instead

The Bernoulli effect

In 1738, the Swiss mathematician Daniel Bernoulli (1700–82) published a book called *Hydrodynamica*, in which he showed that when the speed at which a fluid (liquid or gas) flows increases, the pressure within the flow decreases. He reached this conclusion while studying water flowing through a pipe from a tank where the water level was high to another where it was lower. In the end, of course, the water level is the same in both tanks, but while the water was flowing Bernoulli found the pressure within the flowing stream is related to the speed with which it flows. This is summarized as $p + \frac{1}{2}rV^2$ = a constant, where p is the pressure, r the density of the fluid, and V its velocity (speed).

If, for example, the fluid flows through a tube with a constriction in it, assuming the fluid is not compressed, the rate of flow must increase at the constriction, because the same volume of fluid must pass there in a given time as passes every other point in the tube. It follows from Bernoulli's equation that the pressure must decrease at the constriction. This sounds wrong, but it is what happens and if you perform experiments 6, 7, 8, and 9 in volume 6, these should convince you.

There are several important consequences. The shape of the upper surface of an airplane wing accelerates the air passing over it. This reduces the pressure above the wing and the greater pressure beneath the wing exerts an upward force called *lift*. For the same reason, as wind accelerates when it flows over the shape of a roof pressure falls above the roof, tending to lift it.

It also affects the air flowing into a vortex. Picture this as many very narrow streams. Because of the conservation of angular momentum, the air accelerates as it nears the center of the vortex and the radius of its curved path decreases. Each stream is, therefore, flowing faster than the stream on the side of it away from the center, so pressure within it is lower than that in the adjacent stream. This means that pressure must decrease from the outside to the center of any vortex.

of straight across the base. What Bernoulli found was that when this happens the pressure in the flowing air decreases as it accelerates past the constriction. This exerts an upward force on the roof because the pressure above it is markedly lower than the pressure beneath. Combine this force with the upward force from wind that has penetrated the building from below, and those nails will not hold for long. Once they give and the entire sheet starts to lift, it acts like a sail until it is completely free, then twists and turns chaotically until it falls to the ground.

Tornadoes are most likely to occur along the leading side of an advancing supercell storm. When you see the huge, black or slightly green cloud, with a mass of cloud rotating below part of it, expect a tornado. As it comes nearer, the straight-line wind will increase, often to a force that causes some damage to property. Then the tornado itself arrives, reducing buildings to rubble and hurling debris outward with great force. Within seconds, or at most minutes, the tornado has passed or dissipated, but the rest of the storm is still to come. The wind no longer twists, but behind the tornado lies the gust front where winds reach gale force. Behind them there is the hailstorm, followed by the heaviest of the rain, and all accompanied by lightning. Finally, at the rear of the storm, downcurrents carrying air away from the cloud at ground level produce winds that can reach hurricane speeds. Buildings are exposed to a sequence comprising huge wind gusts, the tornado, severe hail, torrential rain, and winds perhaps of hurricane force, and they may be struck by lightning.

After a storm generating an F-2 tornado, trailer homes will have been shattered and most buildings will have lost their roofs. An F-3 tornado will also demolish some walls, even of well built houses. A violent tornado, F-4 or F-5, will leave very few buildings standing and the debris will be so thoroughly mixed there is no way to tell which rubble belonged to which house. Some houses will have been lifted bodily from their foundations and carried away, only to crash again, not even leaving a pile of ruins as a memorial, because their bricks, mortar, timber, and plaster are likely to have have been carried aloft into the funnel and scattered over a vast area. Some trees will have been stripped of their bark before being torn from the ground. Trains will be overturned, cars thrown hundreds of feet, and, battered by wind and debris, whole areas will have been pounded almost to dust, then drenched by the rain.

Safety during a tornado

In any kind of emergency, ignorance can lead to panic, panic to inappropriate action, and inappropriate action to injury or even death. Your chance of emerging unscathed increases dramatically if you know what to do and calmly carry out a well-rehearsed plan.

Obviously, we cannot anticipate everything that could happen, but it is only common sense to prepare in advance for life-threatening events that may occur. At one time or another tornadoes have occurred in every one of the 50 states, but the risk is not the same everywhere. Oklahoma City, for example, seems to average around three tornadoes a year.

The first step, therefore, is to find out how great the risk is where you live. How often have tornadoes occurred in your area in the past? If there have been several, they could happen again, so be ready for them. If you are new to the neighborhood, check with the nearest office of the National Weather Service or emergency services and if you learn that tornadoes are recognized as a local hazard, find out what plans your community has made. How will people be warned? Where are the safe places to shelter? How would an evacuation be organized?

Your family may not be at home when a tornado strikes. Some members might be at school, others at work or driving. Agree on a place to meet if you are dispersed and cannot return home. Ask a friend who lives a long way away to act as a communication link. If the family is separated, members can telephone the friend to report their position and the friend can pass on the information to the next person who calls. Make sure the friend's number is taped to every telephone in your home and that all of you carry it with you. Naturally, your family can perform the same service for the friend.

Make sure everyone, including young children, knows how to call the emergency services. Make sure all adults and older children know know to turn off the electricity, gas, and water supply.

Know your surrounding area. If there is a "tornado watch" warning, use an up-to-date highway map to plot the location and movement of storms and to plan an escape route if you have to evacuate.

You may be trapped in a shelter for some time, so you will need supplies and should keep them ready. Prepare emergency stores and keep them in or close to where you will shelter. This will be the basement if your home has one, and if not, a small room on the lowest floor such as a bathroom or closet, or a hallway.

Your emergency store should contain supplies for three days. For each person you will need a blanket or sleeping bag, a change of clothing, three gallons of water in airtight containers, and dry or canned food. In addition, your store should have a first aid kit, a battery-powered radio and a flashlight with spare batteries for both, spare car keys, and a few basic tools such as a hammer, screwdrivers, wire cutters, and pliers. If anyone takes prescription medicines, remember to include a supply, and also include any special items needed for infants or elderly or disabled people.

The emergency store should be kept in containers you can carry in case of evacuation. Use suitcases, backpacks, or duffel bags. Check the contents from time to time, and change the water and food every six months.

Keep important family documents in a waterproof wallet somewhere safe but easily accessible. If you have to seek shelter, take them with you. Also take cash or credit cards and personal identification. If you have to leave your home the authorities may not allow you to return unless you can identify yourself.

If there is a "tornado watch" alert, keep the radio or TV on and tuned to a local station for weather updates. Ideally, you should have an NOAA weather radio with a warning alarm. Be ready to switch to battery-powered radio if necessary. Outside, the weather may look fine and everything may be peaceful. The "watch" alert usually covers an area of about 140 miles by 200 miles and you may be perfectly safe, but if the weather looks stormy, start taking precautions. If you are at home, make sure you know where in the house other members of the family are. Shut all windows and exterior doors.

Take warnings of severe thunderstorms seriously. These are issued as a preliminary "watch" followed by a "warning," like those for tornadoes. It is possible for a severe thunderstorm suddenly to develop a mesocyclone and trigger a tornado.

Tornado "warnings" are issued for much smaller areas than "watches." If you hear a warning, it means tornadoes have been seen quite close to you.

Watch the sky from indoors. Expect a tornado if the sky becomes very dark and the cloud seems slightly green or if you see a wall cloud rotating beneath the main cloud. You may hear a loud roar of an approaching tornado. Not all tornadoes are predicted and it is possible that you may see these weather signs without having heard a broadcast warning. Believe what you see. If you delay it may be too late.

Act immediately. If you are at home, gather everyone who is also at home with you and go to the safest place. Keep as far as you can from windows. If possible, shelter beneath a heavy table, workbench, or mattress. If you hear a tornado approaching, have everyone who is not sheltering in this way adopt the safest position. Kneel, then squat on your heels, bend fully forward, and place your hands over the back of your head. If your home is damaged, as soon as it is safe to do so turn off the electricity, gas, and water supplies.

No matter how strongly built you may think it is, or how firmly secured to the ground, no mobile home or trailer is safe. If you are in one when you hear a warning or the sky looks threatening, leave at once. If you are in a trailer park, the owners should have a storm shelter and there should be a warden to pass on warnings and make sure everyone is safe. If there is no designated shelter, seek safety in the open. Go to the lowest ground and if a tornado is coming toward you, lie flat, face down, and cover your head with your hands.

Tornadoes have been known to travel at 70 MPH and they can wreck cars. If you are driving, do not try to outrun one. Stop the car, get out, look for the nearest low ground, and lie face down. If there is a ditch or dry gully or riverbed, lie on the bottom of it and cover your head with your hands.

Workplaces, schools, public buildings, and shopping malls should have designated safe areas and members of staff to see everyone moves to them. Follow the instructions you are given at once, and precisely.

The basement is the safest part of any building. If there is no basement, the refuge will be on the lowest floor, in one or more small rooms or hallways with no external walls. Everyone should be moved away from large, open rooms, such as assembly halls, cafeterias, and gymnasiums. These often have single-span roofs covered with large sheets of exterior skin, and they afford very little protection against a tornado. It may be that engineers have judged the entire building to be unsafe in a tornado. In that case the safest place will be outdoors on the lowest ground and staff members should be available to direct everyone to it.

Do not try to get home if you are at work or in a public building when you hear the warning, and above all, on no account return to your car. Parking lots are especially dangerous places. Schools should keep students on the premises until the danger has passed and they should not be sent home early in an attempt to "beat the storm" if there has been a "tornado watch" alert. They are far safer in school than they would be on the streets or in a school bus.

Planning what you would do in an emergency makes obvious sense. Emergencies are rare, however, and even in the areas most prone to tornadoes they do not happen often. It is easy to grow complacent, neglecting to check your emergency store, for example, or the batteries in your smoke alarms.

Worst of all, perhaps, in the rush of ordinary, everyday life it is easy to forget that not everyone may be familiar with the procedures. From time to time, schools and workplaces hold drills to make sure everyone knows where they should go and that the premises can be evacuated quickly. When you travel by air, your attention will be drawn to the safety instructions and staff may demonstrate the use of life jackets and oxygen masks. It is a routine followed every time a civil airliner sets out on a journey. Ships carrying passengers display safety instructions prominently and in every part of the vessel. Accidents with ships and civil aircraft are also rare events, but this emphasis on safety is a requirement of international maritime and aviation law, and a sensible one. This is what the professionals do and you should be guided by their example.

Check your emergency stores regularly. Make sure the contact number remains displayed close to every telephone. Every so often, make sure every member of your family is familiar with the emergency arrangements. Ask each one directly. Hold drills.

So much attention to things that may never happen may seem excessive. You may find it embarrassing to keep reminding people. Remember, though, that airline staff do not find this repetition (in their case several times a day) embarrassing. They are concerned about saving lives. That should be your aim, too, and experience shows that it works. You can survive a tornado if you have prepared a plan of action and then follow it.

INDEX

Italic numbers indicate ilustrations.